Common Sense Universal Design

Creating Accessible, Safe, Comfortable & Desirable Homes

Common Sense Universal Design

Creating Accessible, Safe, Comfortable & Desirable Homes

Steve Hoffacker
AICP, CAASH, CAPS, CGA, CGP, CMP, CSP, MCSP, MIRM

Common Sense Universal Design

Creating Accessible, Safe, Comfortable & Desirable Homes

Cover photo by Steve Hoffacker.

ALL RIGHTS RESERVED.

© 2013 by Hoffacker Associates LLC
West Palm Beach, Florida, USA

ISBN: 978-0-615-81729-3

―――

This book is written for homeowners, renters, do-it-yourselfers, remodelers, renovators, handymen, health care professionals, architects, and other construction professionals to show how universal design concepts and treatments, that are relatively simple, unobtrusive, functional, comfortable, convenient, contemporary, safe, sensible, accessible, and desirable, can improve the quality of anyone's living space and quality of life — regardless of their age or physical ability.

―――

Books, Articles, Blogs & Other Sales Content By Steve Hoffacker

To access or learn about books, eBooks, articles, blogs, commentary, podcasts, videos, webinars, and other content by Steve Hoffacker for anyone who sells products or services for a living, use the sites below.

"Hoffacker Associates" Website
http://stevehoffacker.com

Steve Hoffacker's Amazon.com Author Page
http://amazon.com/author/stevehoffacker

"Steve Hoffacker's Home Sales Insights" Blog
http://homesalesinsights.com

Steve Hoffacker's "Sales Quips" Blog
http://salesquips.com

"Steve Hoffacker's Success Quips" Blog
http://successquips.com

Steve Hoffacker and Hoffacker Associates can be found online at Facebook, Active Rain, Pinterest, Linked-In, Plaxo, Twitter, Goggle+, YouTube, Tumblr, and other business, real estate, and social sites.

Table Of Contents

Chapter	Page
Preface	11
1. What Is Universal Design?	19
Is Universal Design Real Or A Fad?	19
Why Is There Universal Design?	20
What Qualifies As Universal Design?	21
Why Universal Design Works	23
Isn't This Just Another Name For "ADA"?	24
Who Benefits From Universal Design?	25
2. Universal Design As A Solution	27
The Universal Design Premise	27
"Buying Into" Universal Design	28
The Payoff For Universal Design	29
The Visitability Benefit	31
Where Universal Design Works	31
3. Easy Universal Design Solutions	33
What Makes These Solutions Easy?	33
Lever Door Handles	34

Rocker Light Switches 37
Illuminated Light Switches 38
Motion Sensor Light Switches 38
Photo Cell Light Switches 40
Programmable/Preset Light Switches 41
Digital Thermostats 41
Door/Drawer Pulls 43
Single-Lever Faucets 46
Push Button/Keypad Entry Door Locks 51

4. **More Involved Universal
   Design Solutions** 53

What Makes These Solutions Important? 53
36" Doorways 54
Wider Hallways 58
Door Swing 59
Closet Doors 60
Trench/Forward/Linear Drains 62
Zero-Step/No-Threshold/
   Barrier-Free Showers 65
Shower Glass/Shower Doors 66
Wet Room/Shower Room 69
Bath Temperature Setting/Scald Control 71
Folding Shower Seats 71
Handheld/Personal Showers 73
Towel Bars/Hooks/Rings 75
Strategic Grab Bars 77
Tilt-Out/Tip-Out Sink Front Bins 78
Body Dryer 80
Toe-Kick Lighting 81

Table Of Contents

    Under-Cabinet/Task Lighting 82
    Overhead Lighting 83
    Ceiling Fans 86
    Skylights 87
    Eye-Level Controls 88
    Electrical Outlets 91
    Wall-Mounted Mirrors 92
    Visual Indicators 95

5. Other Universal Design Strategies 97

    Additional Strategies For Safety,
        Convenience, Comfort
        And Accessibility 97
    Contrast And Glare 98
    Flooring 100
    Automatic Dustpan 104
    Room-To-Room Transitions 106
    Motorized Shelving 107
    Kitchen Islands 109
    Modular Sink Base Cabinets 112
    Retractable Sink Base Cabinet Doors 113
    Cabinets And Drawers 115
    Kitchen Desk 119
    Sit-Down Vanity 121
    Up-Front Controls 123
    Easy-Access Appliances 124
    Wall Blocking 127
    Windows 128
    Elevators 131
    Chair Lifts 133
    Back-Up Power 135

6. Universal Design On The Outside 137

Why Look At The Exterior? 137
Zero-Step/Barrier-Free Entrances 138
Lighting 139
Entry Shelves/Tables/Furniture 140
Covered Entry/Guttering 142
Radiant Heating 144
Unloading Area 145
Sidewalks 146

7. Summary Of Universal Design Treatments 149

Universal Design Makes
  A Positive Difference 149
Universal Design Helps
  With Special Needs 151
Universal Design Adds
  Value And Enjoyment 152
Now It's Up To You 153

Preface

This text is available in both printed and Kindle eBook editions.

In fact, it was released first as an eBook to provide quicker access to the information, suggestions, tips, and solutions rather than wait for the print edition to be formatted and prepared.

Both editions are similar in content although there are formatting differences between them. Also, the eBook can be updated as new features or concepts are introduced.

The content in both is a little unusual in that it has been prepared for both the consumer and the professional. Normally a book has one or the other as its audience. Here, the text specifically appeals to both.

If you are a homeowner, renter, building owner, apartment manager, or do-it-yourselfer, you can use the material in this book to evaluate your home or apartment and create modifications for it.

You also can use this information to become aware of the types of changes to your living space that you might want to discuss or consider having done for you by a professional remodeler, contractor, or handyman.

If you are a professional that wants to understand the types of changes and improvements that you can offer your clients and customers, I present sensible modifications that are based on universal design concepts and principles.

In addition to consumers, this book will appeal to remodelers, home builders (although I have a similar book to this one written just for new construction called "Universal Design For Builders"), real estate sales professionals, occupational therapists, physical therapists, case managers, interior designers, architects, durable medical equipment suppliers, trade contractors, caregivers, consultants, engineers, and others.

As I'll talk about in the following text, there are so many opportunities to swap out existing features, fixtures, and devices with something more appropriate. There also are plenty of additional opportunities to create safer, more comfortable, and more convenient living environments — whether you are doing them for your home or apartment or a professional is assisting you.

The concepts in this book are based on several years (and counting) of teaching the Certified Aging-in-Place Specialist ("CAPS") designation program through the National Association of Home Builders, the interactions and contributions of the hundreds of attendees at these programs, my independent research, and the remodeling I have done on my own homes using such products and solutions.

Preface

I have no formal training in architecture or design other than the experience gained in teaching the CAPS program and more than 3 decades of consulting with homebuilders. Nevertheless, the concepts I discuss in this text have been validated by personal experience in the remodeling of my own homes, focus groups with new home buyers over the years, and the concurrence and input of hundreds of attendees at my programs.

You'll find as you read what I have prepared for you that universal design is an intuitive approach that works as an effective solution and strategy for many living environments.

In fact, there are few homes anywhere that couldn't benefit from the use and application of these principles — unless they were designed that way to begin with or have already been modified.

This is not a concept that is just for the United States or for Canada or even North America. This can be applied to homes anywhere in the world.

The universal design approach accommodates a tremendous range of ages, heights, and physical abilities.

For specific physical needs that might require more particular design emphasis and solutions, universal design is still an integral part of the overall approach and a great place to begin because it already allows for a range of heights and physical abilities.

As far as making the changes in your home, much of what we consider to be good universal design — that I have determined on my own and corroborated with the writings of other professionals — are items that you can do on your own if you are so inclined.

Otherwise, these changes can be accomplished easily — and often inexpensively — by remodelers, contractors, carpenters, handymen, or other professionals. Other solutions and changes are a little more substantial and should be incorporated into larger scale remodeling projects.

Please understand that I am not suggesting that anyone's home is somehow deficient or undesirable because it does not include universal design features and elements — or because it doesn't have enough of them or the "right" ones.

However, the more universal design solutions, strategies, or concepts that can be incorporated into the exterior and interior living environment of everyone's home over time, the more it will add to the overall safety and comfort of those living in the homes and the people that are invited into or choose to visit them.

Also, the ideas and strategies presented here are based on technology and solutions currently available. It is entirely likely that new products and solutions or even best practices will become available that meet the definition and spirit of universal design and how it is

Preface

delivered that should be considered for use as they become known.

The central theme of this text is creating safer living environments with virtually invisible changes — by adding universal design elements or replacing existing features and components with more accessible ones.

The improvements, solutions, and design strategies I present in this book — without respect to any particular age group or any specific needs — are those treatments that can be accomplished without looking much different from what they are replacing.

The key is improvements that are essentially invisible — ones that do call attention to themselves. For instance, If wheelchair access — over and above what is suggested as universal design treatments for entrances, hallways, and interior doorways — was created by eliminating base cabinets under sinks or cooktops when there is no wheelchair access required, that might look visibly out-of-place to a casual visitor and call attention to the design.

While you might want this design incorporated into your home because you like the idea of this design — even when a current or foreseeable need is not present — universal design solutions are those that don't suggest how or by whom the space is to be used.

Nevertheless, a wall-mounted or pedestal sink in the powder room or secondary bath or a roll-under countertop or eating area on an island or peninsula would accomplish the same purpose and fit right into any design.

Similarly, grab bars or railings lining the hallway or other walls in the home would call attention to this design element and give an institutional look to many homes — especially when they aren't required for use by the current residents.

However, a chair rail (not a dowel or closet rod), that is wide enough in thickness to provide some support or because it can be grasped by someone who needs it, just fits right in without calling any special attention to the design.

This book is not intended to address every single area of the home but will provide many solid ideas and strategies on ways to make nearly anyone's home more accessible, comfortable, attractive, convenient, and safe — whether you are doing this for your own home or you are the provider or designer for a client's home.

Common Sense Universal Design

Creating Accessible, Safe, Comfortable & Desirable Homes

1

What Is Universal Design?

Is Universal Design Real Or A Fad?

Universal design may seem like a fad since it is relatively new and has a large and growing following, but it is real — and it is here to stay.

It makes sense and it offers a very practical solution and strategy for increasing the safety, comfort, convenience, and accessibility for everyone, regardless of what type of living spaces you have — inside the dwelling as well as around the home and yard on the exterior.

Therefore, it seems to be the real deal.

It's because it offers safe, practical, comfortable, intuitive, unobtrusive, contemporary solutions and styles that I embrace it. I think you will want to as well

— for your personal residences and for those of anyone you help to achieve this objective.

This seems to be much too practical to be a passing trend or fad. Its value is borne out in what it provides.

Why Is There Universal Design?

There may be many good reasons or explanations for universal design to be used in America and elsewhere around the world, but as far as I am concerned, the aging of the population is why it is getting so much attention now. Certainly all of us are aging.

Of course, none of us likes to think of ourselves as getting older or "aging" so we have to approach it from a different perspective.

Aging is a sensitive issue, but universal design is a sensible way of approaching it.

The idea of "aging-in-place" or remaining in your home for as long as you choose and as long as you are able to remain somewhat independent is at the heart of the universal design concept. There is so much to be said for maintaining one's independence.

Rather than approach the idea of aging in place, however, I prefer the notion of people staying in the homes that they love for as long as they desire.

At some point in your life, you will find a home that you like, that you are comfortable living in, that generally provides for your needs (or can be adapted to do so), and is in a neighborhood or location that you like.

You might already have found that home and are living in it right now, or you might be searching for it.

If you think you might have one or two more moves left before you find that home you want to remain in indefinitely, then your current home just might be the perfect home for someone else that needs to find their home that they want to stay in for as long as they like.

In that sense, making universal design and accessibility improvements in your current home — even though you might be planning on moving — could add value to it, give it broader appeal, and be just right for someone else who might really appreciate the improvements you have made — and be willing to pay for them.

In the meantime, if you were to make the types of improvements I am discussing and presenting in this text, you could enjoy the benefits of a safer, more accessible design.

What Qualifies As Universal Design?

Universal design solutions, components, strategies, concepts, and elements are those that appeal to the widest possible audience — regardless of age, physical size, height, weight, or ability.

With the exception of those individuals that require specific design applications for their particular needs and abilities, universal design generally serves quite well for the normal aging process and for those who have various special access needs.

Essentially, universal design must appeal to and be usable and accessible to the general population without qualification. That's what makes it universal.

In 1997, North Carolina State University formulated seven principles of universal design. Thus, we now have a measure for determining what is and what is not considered to be within the realm of what we are discussing.

Basically, universal design solutions, fixtures, features, elements, and devices must be accessible and usable by the general population without any advance knowledge or instruction in how to operate something (such as turning on a faucet or light switch or opening a door).

In addition, the solutions and fixtures must be so easy and flexible or forgiving to use that a person doesn't have to operate them perfectly or "just-so" in order to make them work effectively.

They must be installed or located in such a way that nearly everyone can reach and use them.

It should require a minimum of effort and not depend on any particular height, hand or arm strength, gripping or grasping ability, or range-of-motion.

When used correctly and appropriately, universal design elements fit seamlessly into the living space and become just part of the home without calling attention to the design or sticking out in anyway as something special or unusual.

Being unobtrusive is a major design objective.

Why Universal Design Works

In addition to being unobtrusive and just fitting into the normal living environment — whether they are plumbing fixtures, cabinets, countertops, doors, hardware, faucets, switches, controls, lighting, or other elements — they actually enhance the appearance and value of the home.

Putting in such items as a single-lever faucet, a lever door handle, or a rocker light switch (all of which I will talk about in more detail in Chapter 3) makes the home safer for you, makes controls easier to operate, makes it more convenient for you and your visitors or guests, modernizes the look of your home, and adds value to your home since people interested in purchasing your home at a later date would look for and expect to find such features included.

Thus, your home looks more attractive, more inviting (for guests or visitors to come to your home and feel welcome), safer, more convenient, more comfortable, and more contemporary (with up-to-date features).

Isn't This Just Another Name For "ADA"?

"ADA" or the "Americans With Disabilities Act" dictates what must be addressed and in what manner to make indoor spaces and entrances accessible to everyone — especially people using a wheelchair or other forms of mobility assistance.

Universal design solutions, components, strategies, and elements are complementary to that ideal in many ways.

Nevertheless, single family homes, duplexes, triplexes, and quads are exempt from the provisions of ADA although some local building codes could require some compliance.

Designing to comply with ADA requirements may make good sense, and much of what I mention or discuss in this text is consistent with ADA guidelines. Universal design and ADA are not the same thing, however.

Who Benefits From Universal Design?

Essentially everyone can benefit from universal design ideals, strategies, and solutions. That's why it has the name universal attached to it.

In writing this book, I choose to appeal to homeowners and renters (tenants) who want to know about good universal design. If that describes you, then I want you to be able to incorporate such design considerations into your remodeling or updating plans.

You might be contemplating doing the work yourself, or you might be discussing it with a professional that you will engage to do all or part of it.

If you are that designer, remodeler, handyman, or contractor who is going to be consulted and enlisted to do the renovations, I want you to be prepared with the design changes and solution that you can offer your clients.

If you are an occupational therapist, physical therapist, another type of health care professional, electrician, plumber, carpenter, real estate sales professional, home stager, electrical service contractor (ESC), durable medical equipment (DME) specialist, home inspector, architect, HVAC contractor, appliance retailer, tile setter, cement mason, flooring contractor, flatwork contractor, or structural engineer, you likely will be involved in helping to make people's homes safer, more comfortable, more convenient, more contemporary, more accessible, and more valuable.

Therefore, you should be aware of these universal design solutions and treatments also.

Because universal design is meant to accommodate the widest range of ages and abilities, it is not driven by someone's specific physical ability or medical condition. As such, all members of the household can avail themselves of the solutions.

There are many needs-specific solutions that are available, but this text focuses on universal design — products, solutions, strategies, and modifications to appeal to the broadest audience possible and offer a safe, convenient, comfortable, and accessible living environment.

In addition, universal design is not limited to just owner occupied residences. Depending on the extent and complexity of the design changes desired, many of the strategies I present in this text are appropriate for renters as well.

2

Universal Design As A Solution

The Universal Design Premise

If you accept the premise that universal design really is for all ages and abilities, it means that it will accommodate the reach, hand and arm strength, range-of-motion, coordination, and physical abilities of a child (say a 4-, 5-, or 6-year old) as well as a 90-year old, and someone who is normally ambulatory to someone who typically uses a walker or wheelchair for assistance.

It follows then that universal design is the preferred design strategy and course of action for creating and modifying living spaces for essentially everyone.

Universal design permits accessibility and use of the various aspects of your home — inside and out— in a safe, friendly, comfortable, and convenient manner without any adaptation or other considerations.

There may be special modifications required to address specific needs in your home, but using the concepts and strategies of universal design will give most people a safer, more comfortable quality of life — regardless of age or physical ability. Moreover, the changes will hardly be noticeable.

Over time, the universal design changes that can be made will be even more beneficial from a safety, convenience, and comfort basis.

Remember as you look at solutions and strategies in this text that we are talking about things that work for nearly everyone irrespective of their physical age, height, weight, or ability.

Also, it doesn't matter whether you are standing or seated, with full range-of-motion or some limitations, having unrestricted mobility or some mobility issues, with no stamina or coordination issues or moderate ones, and even with moderate cognitive issues.

In short, universal design offers accessibility, safety, and convenience to all.

"Buying Into" Universal Design

As a homeowner or tenant considering universal design changes for your personal residence, you need to sign on to having these improvements made in your home or apartment. This is true whether you are contemplating doing part or all of the work yourself or you are going to have it done by a remodeler and other professionals.

As professionals who might do this in your own home or for your clients, you need to embrace the positive benefits that these solutions provide.

There are six major reasons for wanting and consenting to have universal design strategies and solutions implemented in your home or those of people you are working with: safety, comfort, convenience, accessibility, marketability, and visitability.

Any one of these reasons would be sufficient for going ahead with universal design solutions, but most people will benefit from the majority of them.

The Payoff For Universal Design

Safety is a key objective in remodeling a home or apartment, and universal design definitely improves safety.

The reason that universal design elements result in more safety is because they provide more lighting, easier opening drawers and doors, more stable footing and standing surfaces (inside and outside), easier to use controls, better hygiene, and other helpful solutions.

They also provide convenience, comfort, and economic benefits, but mostly they make your living spaces safer.

By making things more accessible and easier to use, generally they are more convenient to use and more enjoyable — regardless of how tall someone is, whether they are seated or standing, or what their range-of-motion or other limitations or concerns might be.

You can be more comfortable and confident with setting the temperature, using various fixtures and appliances, using water at a pleasant and safe temperature, accessing controls without having to reach for them or stretch to see what the settings are, and generally moving about in your home.

In terms of marketability, universal design changes and improvements can make your home easier to sell or rent because it will appeal to a broader section of the population and have more actual value or more perceived value — achieving a higher sales price or rent and fewer days on the market.

Think in terms of modernizing your home or living space, making it more contemporary, using newer technology, and achieving more style — in addition to just making the changes because of the safety, convenience, or comfort benefits. There is a real economic and aesthetic benefit to making universal design changes.

The Visitability Benefit

A big reason for incorporating universal design changes into your home is for visitability. This may be an unfamiliar term for you, but it has to do will the ability — or inability — of anyone to visit your home or apartment comfortably and conveniently.

Whenever you entertain or host a meeting, party, get-together, or discussion group, you want people to feel welcome in coming to your home without wondering if they will feel comfortable.

You won't always know in advance whether someone can climb steps or negotiate a narrow entryway — when that is the case. Therefore, you want to make your home as "visitable" as possible — capable of being entered and navigated without restrictions or limitations by whomever you invite or comes along with someone else you invited.

Where Universal Design Works

To achieve greater safety inside and around your home, to offer more comfort and convenience to you and the people who live in your home with you (as well as those who visit on occasion), and to enhance the value and resale potential of your home, there are many things that can be done — starting with those that are relatively simple and inexpensive that often can be done without a building permit, inspection, or any demolition or construction.

In fact, other than knowing that something has been added, moved, or removed, no one will ever know any work was done. The next day, it will look like it has always been that way.

So we'll start with those easy fixes that involve switches, drawer pulls, door knobs, and lighting.

Then we'll move on from there to items that are going to require some construction.

No area of the home is going to be exempt from the changes I am suggesting, but the kitchen and bath areas will receive the most attention.

These are, after all, the areas where people tend to spend a lot of their time and the areas that people value the most when shopping for a new home.

Existing plumbing fixtures, major appliances, flooring, cabinetry, windows, wall mounted controls, electric outlets, towel bars, mirrors, and similar items will be addressed — along with things such as grab bars, other kitchen and bathroom features, auxiliary lighting, and items for the exterior of your home.

3

Easy Universal Design Solutions

What Makes These Solutions Easy?

There are several changes that can be made in an existing home — or a new home as it is being designed or before it is completed — to make it more comfortable, safe, convenient, or accessible that require nothing more than taking out what is there (or what is planned in the case of new construction) and replacing it with a more suitable product or item. Essentially anyone can do it.

As a homeowner or renter, you or someone in your family can do it. A handyman can do it. A remodeler, contractor, or builder can do it.

These changes make a big, noticeable improvement, but they require no building permit or inspection. A little care is required, but they are pretty easy to accomplish — depending on who does them and how many are undertaken at one time.

These modifications will cover aspects of electrical, plumbing, lighting, doors, and cabinets.

Some other changes that I suggest as we go along will require some light construction and may mean a little dust, localized mess, and temporary disruption in a particular room or area of the home.

You just need to make sure that whoever does the work in your home — besides you or someone you know and trust very well — that it is a properly authorized and licensed activity for the person performing the work.

Lever Door Handles

When I think of universal design, lever door handles are one of the first items that comes to mind.

These are the epitome of universal design. This concept truly works for all ages and abilities and provides safety, comfort, and convenience.

The use of the lever style door handle on all doors that open in or out — including storm doors, screen doors, entrance doors, patio doors, and interior doors, both with and without locks — allow the very young and the very old to use them successfully.

This includes young people who are so short as to be barely able reach the handles with outstretched fingers to those with weakened hand or arm strength or severe range-of-motion limitations who may have difficulty extending their hands or using their fingers to grasp things such as a traditional door knob.

What makes the lever handle such an ideal universal design element is the way it can be operated and the door released to open in several different ways. It has a large tolerance for error and low physical effort.

It can be used with the full hand to grasp it, just a couple of fingers to push down on it, the side of the hand (open or in a fist) to push on it, the back of the hand or wrist to push down, the elbow or forearm to push down, the sides of both hands together to apply enough release pressure when your hands are messy or when you're holding something that you can't put down easily, or even with a box or something else you might be holding to push down on the lever.

This obviously accommodates the full range of ages and many different types of physical abilities, but it has the added practical benefit of being able to be operated when your hands are full with something you really don't want to set down or can't put down easily — or when your hands might be messy or greasy and you'd rather not grasp the lever and then have to go back later and clean it.

From a safety standpoint, the levers (unlike traditional rounded knobs) can be operated successfully while wearing a heavy glove or mitten or while using a towel to prevent transfer of whatever you might have on your hands.

From an aesthetic standpoint, the lever handles provide a nice sleek, clean, modern look and are available in several styles, finishes, and colors — with and without locks.

For those that want an immediate solution without replacing every door knob in the home, the rounded knobs can be fitted with a device — also available in various colors and finishes — that adapts the knobs to look and function like a lever handle.

A lockset and door handle that is the opposite of universal design and accessibility is the thumb-latch style entry lockset that requires sometimes tremendous thumb pressure or pressing down with the side of your hand to depress the latch enough and then hold it long enough to disengage it from the striker plate and jamb.

This is often a two-handed operation — depressing the latch with one hand and holding it that way while grasping the handle and pulling or pushing the door open with the other — and presents challenges to many people in using it. There is not much tolerance for error in using this.

Rocker Light Switches

I also think of the rocker or "Decora" light switches when I think of universal design. These and the lever door handles top the list.

Literally, anyone who can reach or touch this style of light switch can use it. Both the door handle and the light switch offer a component of safety, comfort, and convenience in being able to use them so flexibly. Both require low physical effort and can accommodate a wide tolerance for error.

You can push on the light switch in the middle or on any other part of it. It will turn on or off, as needed.

You can use one finger, the tip of a finger, the flat of your hand, a fist, the side of your hand, the back of your hand, your wrist, your elbow, your shoulder, or even an object that you might be holding in your hand — basically anything that provides enough contact and pressure to move the switch into the on or off position.

Again, if you are holding something or your hands are dirty and you don't want to make a mark on the switch, switchplate, or wall, the rocker or Decora switch is great.

Contrast this with the tiny toggle-style switch that typically must be grasped or pushed with more physical effort and with greater accuracy that the rocker switches — there is no comparison.

In terms of aesthetics, the rocker or Decora switches provide a clean, modern, contemporary look, while the toggle switches look a little old-fashioned.

The rocker switches are a great universal design solution, but in many ways they are just the accepted style to use. They definitely fit in and are probably more noticeable today when they aren't used than when they are.

Illuminated Light Switches

As long as we are talking light switches, they can be obtained in the rocker or Decora style with a small light in them that makes them easy to find in dim light or at night. Simply take out the existing switches and replace them with these.

This adds safety and convenience — plus the comfort of knowing that the light switch can be located.

Motion Sensor Light Switches

In swapping out light switches from toggle to rocker or Decora — or even if the rocker or Decora switches are already in place — a motion sensor (also called motion detector) light switch that mounts in the same space as the switch it is replacing can provide peace-of-mind and added safety as well as convenience in low traffic areas.

The switch turns on any light that is controlled by it — ceiling fixture or lamp with incandescent, florescent, LED, or halogen bulbs — and stays on for either a fixed period of time or for a time that can be set to turn off the lights after the sensor detects no movement in the room.

When you enter a darkened room — such as a powder room or guest bedroom — with something in your hands to put away in that room (paper goods, towels, linens, or clean laundry) you can take care of your mission without being concerned about locating or using the light switch. This works great for visitors and guests also.

This also provides a measure of security by having lights that come on as if someone in the home has turned them on — when someone or something not expected to be present is detected.

A similar idea with less flexibility than having a light come on when you enter a room and turn off when you leave is to use an electric timer that plugs into an electrical outlet. It allows one or more lamps to plug into it and be turned on and off at fixed times that you determine and set. This works well for holiday or decorative lighting also.

For exterior lighting, fixtures are available that are solar powered so they literally can be place anywhere — on the fascia, on a pole, on a fence, on a porch railing or post, on the garage — without needing electric wiring to run them.

They are operated by a motion sensor and powered by solar energy. The solar collectors just need to be mounted where they get direct sunlight during the day to recharge (see page 140 for more).

Photo Cell Light Switches

This is another alternative for exterior lighting and indoor lamps that only need to be on at night.

This strategy adds safety, comfort, and convenience to the living space.

A photo cell that is part of the light fixture or a separate sensor switch that is screwed into the light socket with the bulb then screwed into it will turn the lights on that it controls when the ambient lighting has dropped to a low enough level to require the lights to come on.

They will stay on until sufficient daylight causes them to turn off. However, they sometimes will come on and remain on when the sky is very cloudy or during a heavy rain or snowfall.

The important thing to remember is to aim the photo cell sensors away from other lights that might interfere with their sensory ability and to generally have exterior sensors facing north or east.

Programmable/Preset Light Switches

This is another safety, convenience, and efficiency option available.

Whether the lights come on with a sensor or are turned on manually, a device that still fits into a standard switch box can use preset times that come with the switch for the light or lights controlled by the switch to remain on for a fixed period of time (for instance 5 or 10 minutes).

It also can be programmed by you to stay on for a certain period of time before turning off the lights.

For any of these devices that I have discussed for controlling when the lights come on or turn off, there are several manufacturers, models, styles, sources, and price points available.

Digital Thermostats

This solution is similar to the light switch improvements for additional convenience and comfort, and it allows anyone in the home to access and use the device.

That's what makes it universal.

It's just a matter of taking out a manual, dial-type or slide-switch style mercury thermostat and replacing it with one that has a digital display — programmable or not.

Some thermostats have the ability to set and control temperatures for various times of the day or for multiple days. Some just maintain the temperature as it is set — for heating or cooling.

Either way, they can be read from a few feet away and don't rely on grasping a dial or switch and trying to move it a small amount. Some can even be controlled remotely from smartphones and tablets.

Obviously, this is good for all ages and even people with some vision difficulties.

It is certainly much easier to read the display with a specific temperature number than trying to determine the settings and temperature on a non-digital one since the numbers are larger and are usually lit on the digital type — it's also easier to set the precise desired temperature.

This is easily changed out by you as the homeowner or renter, but it also can be done by a handyman or remodeler as part of a larger project.

It can be replaced exactly where is has been, but an even better strategy is to move it to a lower position so it is more accessible and visible to everyone.

This will require a little more work to move the wiring so the first step would be just to replace the old thermostat with a digital one. Then it can be lowered later to a more accessible position.

Door/Drawer Pulls

Opening doors and drawers throughout the home may be an issue for people with small hands, weak hand strength, or arthritis in their hands or fingers. They may have trouble grasping and using the door and drawer pulls or handles.

In order to make it easier for everyone to use them, this one universal design change can make a huge difference.

In addition to making it easier, more comfortable, and safer for everyone to use, replacing the door and drawer knobs and pulls can really dress up the appearance of a kitchen or bath and give it a modern look.

Depending on which hardware is selected and the number of cabinet drawers and doors in the kitchen, baths, laundry room, garage, basement, and elsewhere in the home, it may not be an inexpensive change but one that is easily done.

This certainly can be done by homeowners and renters. It also can be done by a handyman or during a kitchen or bath makeover.

What you want to achieve are door and drawer handles and pulls that require little-to-no gripping strength to operate — unlike that needed for using small knobs that have to be grasped before they can be leveraged to open the door or drawer.

The pulls can easily be switched out by removing the existing ones and using the same mounting holes — if they have two posts that are 3" apart.

Pulls that require wider mounting holes than 3" will require drilling new holes and possibly patching and touching up the existing ones.

For the knobs that have just a single mounting bolt, a second hole (or sometimes two holes to achieve a center alignment) will need to be drilled.

This is easily done by creating a template out of paper, cardboard, or thin wood to get all of the holes in the same place on the various doors and drawer fronts.

Again, some patching and touchup might be required.

The more space between the actual drawer or door pull and the drawer or door surface the better so that more of someone's hand can engage the pull and there is more tolerance for using it effectively.

The major safety concern for existing and new pulls is that any material on the pull surface that sticks out past the main part of the pull can catch clothing or skin when someone walks by too closely or comes in contact with it.

An alternate to using door pulls is to use magnetic latches that hold a door closed and then release it by depressing the lock slightly with the door front to "pop" it open.

Some doors also will remain closed with tension or spring assisted hinges or just the weight of the door without a catch — and open by grasping a corner or edge of the door and gently pulling on it. Such doors typically do not have a door pull and provides a cleaner, more uniform look that way.

The issue with doors that have no pulls on them — or don't use pulls to release the latch and open the doors — is that they aren't as intuitive to use and may be confusing for guests or visitors.

Someone has to initially determine if they need to push on the door or attempt to grasp an edge and pull it open — assuming they have enough hand and arm strength or manual dexterity to be able to grasp the edge of a door and pull it open.

Also, figuring out where to push on the door to release it may take a few attempts — along the top edge or the side, in the middle or towards one corner?

Single-Lever Faucets

When I think of universal design, another one of the first items that comes to mind is the single-lever faucet — for safety, comfortable application, accessibility, and convenience.

Again, this is a classic example of universal design. It truly works for all ages and abilities, and it's already included in many homes just because it looks nice.

As a homeowner or renter, you can easily swap out any existing dual-style or two-handle faucet set with the single-lever model if you have the tools and experience to do light plumbing work.

The important thing to remember is removing all the residue and gaskets or putty from the existing installation and putting the new one in place on a clean, dry surface — using the new gaskets and putty as recommended in the instructions that come with the new faucet.

Of course, handymen, remodelers, or plumbers can do this as part of a larger project.

Just make sure the replacement faucet uses the same holes that are already present in the sink or countertop or that it completely covers and seals any of the unused ones. Don't leave any holes exposed.

The single-lever faucet is more stylish and contemporary than two-handle faucets, although fancy and rather expensive two-handle faucet sets can be purchased.

That really isn't the point — how fancy or expensive they are. Aside from offering a sleek, modern look, the single-lever faucet offers significant safety benefits over the two-handle style.

The single-lever faucet can be operated by anyone who can reach it without being overly concerned about someone accidently burning or hurting themselves by getting hot water unexpectedly.

The faucet handle and mixer would have to be positioned to the far left and have the hot water come on rather instantly for this to be a concern.

Contrast that with someone using a sink with two faucet handles and not paying attention, realizing, or understanding that the left side is the hot water control and being indifferent to the water temperature as long as they were able to have water coming out — until it may be too late to avoid discomfort or a mild burn.

A safety benefit that the single-lever faucet affords that likely everyone can appreciate and relate to is being able to use it while you are preparing food.

After handling raw meat or fish or having sauces or something sticky or messy on your hands, you can turn on the faucet and have the water come on without needing to touch the handle with your affected hands. There are several other ways of activating the lever without grabbing it.

The same is true from doing other work around the house or yard that might leave your hands dirty, oily, muddy, or greasy.

Depending on the type and size of the lever, you can turn on the faucet with your forearm, fist, wrist, back of your hands, elbows, your hands while wearing kitchen gloves or using a towel you are holding to avoid direct contact, a wooden spoon or other kitchen utensil, or even a bowl or pot you might be holding.

There are many ways to activate the faucet without actually grasping the handle because it is so flexible — a hallmark of universal design.

There also are faucets available now that just require some type of light contact along the spout to activate the water flow — less intuitive but very convenient.

Generally, the water temperature is more consistent with a single-lever faucet than the two-handle system when the water is turned off and then back on again because the temperature mixing does not have to be redone.

Although the water is subject to cooling off depending on the length of time that has passed since turning off the single-lever faucet, the water is relatively the same temperature as it was when it was turned off (or it soon will be as soon as it heats back up).

With a two-handle faucet system, the water has to be remixed by turning on each handle and then testing the water temperature until it feels about the way it was previously — unless it had been turned on with only cold or only hot water.

This is another safety and convenience benefit of using the single-lever faucet.

Another universal design gadget that you may want to get or request — for those spouts that will accept them — is a screw-on adapter in the place of a typical aerator that provides a blue light or red light to the water stream to indicate its relative temperature.

This is an immediate visual clue for the general water temperature as well as great fun for kids and a conversation starter when guests are present.

Another option is selecting a faucet that already has a built-in light to indicate the relative temperature.

Single-lever faucets should be used throughout the home — kitchens, baths, laundry rooms, mud rooms, garages, summer kitchens, patios, and basements.

One additional safety, comfort, and convenience issue to remember involves the choice of the faucet spout to provide enough room to get your hands under the flowing water and also to reduce splashing and spray.

Some faucets have very short spouts, and it is hard to get your hands or a dish or pot totally under the water without contacting the back of the sink.

Make sure the water is delivered a comfortable distance away from the back of the sink.

Another faucet spout consideration is excess spray or splash from a spout that is too high (resulting in a lot of splash or water bounce off the bottom of the sink to the surrounding countertop, floor, or whoever is using the sink) or angled to the point that water tends to hit the bottom of the sink and refract directly out onto the person using it.

Both cases present safety, comfort, and convenience issues.

Shallow bowls and vessel sinks (because of their shape) tend to create more splash issues than others.

Push Button/Keypad Entry Door Locks

Here is a practical solution that affords additional safety and convenience.

Replace existing entry door locksets with a push button or keypad lock system.

Make sure to get a lockset with a lever handle.

Simply take the lockset out that is there and replace it with the keypad lockset. There are different colors and finishes available.

This design works for all ages.

If you have young children who can be trusted with the combination, they can unlock the door by pressing the correct numbers or letters. There is no worry of them losing a key or for you trying to keep track of how many people have been issued keys.

Everyone in the household can unlock the door by just punching in the correct combination, and the lock can be reprogrammed as often as desired for additional security. This is great for family that may visit regularly but not live at your address.

Remembering a combination could be an issue with people who have short-term memory loss, but then using a key to unlock the door is likely an issue as well.

An additional safety and security benefit of the keypad lock is that it can be programmed with a separate combination for temporary access each time repair and service technicians or personnel need to enter the home — so that the actual combination is not handed out or revealed and there is no need to have a key given to them or hidden outside for them.

4

More Involved Universal Design Solutions

What Makes These Solutions Important?

In addition to the several changes we just looked at that require hardly any work in your home other than swapping out less efficient or effective light switches, door handles, cabinet and drawer handles and pulls, and faucets, there are several changes that can be made in an existing home — or a new home as it is being designed or completed — to make it more comfortable, safe, convenient, or accessible (and even valuable) that require some advance planning and some professional help.

Unless you are very skilled in doing some of this work yourself as a homeowner, you are going to require the help of contractors to help you accomplish the design strategies and solutions that I discuss in this chapter.

Some construction and demolition will likely be required to complete these changes. That's why it may take the work of professionals to accomplish it.

Nevertheless, these are the types of solutions and changes that you should consider as part of a comprehensive, sensible universal design approach to creating a safe, comfortable, and accessible home.

Depending on the complexity of the changes and the extent of them, they might be able to be accomplished without a building permit or inspection.

These changes will make a big, noticeable impact on the general safety and comfort of your living space. However, in keeping with the objective of universal design of having the changes as invisible as possible, they won't necessarily be obvious to those not familiar with the way your home looked previously.

36" Doorways

This is another one of the items that tops my list when I think of universal design.

It is such an intuitive solution, but it has yet to be embraced by the majority of the nation's homebuilders.

If more homes came with 36" doorways already included, homeowners would not have to incur the time, expense, and inconvenience (regardless of who does the work) of replacing the existing doors with larger ones.

Unless 36" (or "3-0" as it's called for 3'-0") interior doorways are specifically requested by new home purchasers in semi-custom or custom homes, most of the new homes being built are designed with 32" or smaller doorways (called "2-8" in construction terminology for 2'-8" or 32").

The difference in wall space between a 32" and 36" doorway is 4", but that is a very important 4" for universal design and accessibility.

The practical reason for all interior doorways being 36" wide — many exterior doorways already are 36" (or larger when double doors are used) — is for ease of moving furniture about in the home.

Anyone who has ever moved a mattress or bed frame into a bedroom — or other furniture from room-to-room in a home or apartment — knows how challenging it can be dealing with a 32" or smaller doorway compared to one that is 36".

Skinned knuckles, bruised shins, and dinged furniture — or even getting furniture stuck or wedged into the doorway opening — have resulted from narrow doorways.

It's sometimes hard enough with 36" doorways, but that is so much better than smaller ones.

Just for giving everyone an easier time of moving furniture or other items about between rooms in the home or apartment is reason enough for have the wider doorways.

The visitability factor comes into play when we note that a wheelchair may need 29" or more of clearance — with a 32" width being the published design guideline — just to negotiate safely through a doorway.

While a 32" doorway is wide enough in theory, it doesn't measure up. Taking into account a door thickness of 1⅜" or more, a hinge of another ¾" or so, and the stop (nearly another ⅜"), the effective clearance in a 32" doorway has been reduced by some 2½" or more.

In order to achieve a true 32" or larger effective passageway for easy wheelchair access in a home, 36" doors are the minimum size that should be used. A few inches wider would be even better, but 36" doorways are currently the widest size commonly available.

In some cases, pocket doors — mounted inside the walls — or sliding doors (also called "barn doors") — hung along the inside or outside walls of the doorway — may provide a wider effective opening as well.

Mounting inside the walls will require some demolition and construction — and possible moving of electric wiring and light switches.

Surface mounted doors do not require any major construction — just installing the track and hanging the door along with removing the stop, striker plate, hinges, and casing from the door jamb and then patching as required to leave a smooth opening. This may be a larger job than you are willing to tackle on your own, and a handyman or remodeler can be used.

To swap out the 32" or smaller door with the 36" door, it's often just a matter of removing the 32" ("2-8") or smaller doorway (door, jamb, and molding), enlarging the opening, and then replacing it with a larger one — making sure it is plumb and square so it opens freely.

The drywall needs to be trimmed — or cutout and then replaced, patched, and painted to allow for a wider opening — and the doorway needs to be reframed to make this happen. Wiring and light switches may have to be moved as well.

This can be a do-it-yourself project but is more easily accomplished by a handyman, carpenter, or remodeling contractor.

For doorways at the end of hallways that cannot be enlarged without first making the hallways wider, this should be done by a remodeler when undertaking a more comprehensive project.

To widen the hallways, the space will need to be taken from the rooms bordering the hallway.

Wider Hallways

This idea goes along with 36" doorways but takes a lot more planning and work to accomplish.

This is not a matter of just removing a door and making the opening larger. We are talking about moving walls — at least one and likely two or more.

A typical interior hallway in a home is 36" or less, and that obviously can't accommodate a 36" doorway at the end of the hallway or comfortable passage along the hallway by anyone in a wheelchair or walker.

To make hallways wider, the rooms with a common wall with the hallway will necessarily be affected.

Widening hallways requires tearing out existing walls and reconstructing them a few inches away from where they were and toward the adjacent space. Some wiring and possibly air conditioning or heating ductwork will have to be relocated also.

The ceiling and flooring in the hallway will need to be redone or repaired as the space is widened into the original wall area where no ceiling or floor treatment existed (the walls were there).

Hallways that are 42-45" in width seem to be field-tested and reasonable. Adding wall blocking (adaptable design) inside the hallway walls as they are rebuilt will facilitate installation of grab bars at a later date as a needs-specific solution.

This project will likely require the services of a handyman, remodeler, HVAC contractor, electrician, painter, and flooring contractor — and a dumpster or some other way of removing the construction debris.

Door Swing

Occasionally, existing interior or exterior doors are mounted so that they open from the wrong side or in the wrong direction for the convenience, safety, and accessibility of those in the household — meaning the hinges need to be switched left-for-right or right-for-left — due to the amount of room near the latch or door handle side of the door and the room to approach it and open it easily.

It could also be a matter of what the door opens into or onto in terms of floor area near the door, an adjacent wall, cabinets, fixtures, or furniture.

Reversing the swing from side to side, so that it opens opposite of where it is now but still in or out the same, requires a little work in terms of reversing the position of the hinges and striker plate and recess — plus patching, sanding, and painting where the hardware was before being moved.

Reversing whether the door opens in or out (except where local building codes require certain doors to open a particular way) requires a little more work because the stop and lockset have to be reversed also.

Unless you are particularly handy with woodworking, this is likely a job for professionals such as a handyman, carpenter, or a remodeling contractor.

Closet Doors

There are many different styles of closet doors, depending on what room the closet is located in and what the purpose of the closet is.

There are bedroom closets — both wall closets with bypass, hinged, or bi-fold doors as well as walk-in closets with pocket, bi-fold, or hinged doors.

There are linen, coat, and utility closets in the hallway or foyer. There are linen closets in the bath. There is the pantry and possibly laundry closet space in the kitchen (sometimes the hallway).

The same comments about door swing apply to closets in terms of accessibility and ease of use.

An additional consideration is that the door must remain open while the closet is in use rather than just being opened to pass through it or closed for privacy like other doors in the home.

Therefore you need to take a hard look at how each door is used before deciding if they need to be changed or allowed to remain,

Evaluate the approach space to make sure that it is safe and adequate, look at the way the door is opened and the impact it has on adjacent space or furniture while it remains in the open position, see if there are any potential obstructions preventing the door from opening fully or allowing others in the home to walk past it while it is open, and assess how easy it is to open and close the door to gain access to the closet.

For in-line pantry and linen closets that are part of the cabinetry, dividing the space into smaller compartments with smaller doors is better so that the doors aren't so heavy and that just one area of the closet or pantry can be accessed as needed rather than opening a large door to the entire space.

Again, if you are particularly handy with woodworking some of this can be accomplished by the homeowner, but this is likely a job for professionals such as a handyman, kitchen and bath designer, or a remodeling contractor.

Trench/Forward/Linear Drains

In a traditional bathtub — with or without a fixed shower head installation or handheld shower — the drain is located forward. It is at the end of the tub — typically under the fill spout and the faucet handles or mixer and at the end opposite of where someone typically steps into the tub.

However, in a stall shower — either manufactured or constructed on site — the drain in the shower pan is located in or near the middle. The floor of the shower is formed into an inverse pyramid with the drain at the center.

Even when the floor of the shower is formed without using a manufactured pan, it is still constructed with the same design and shape.

I think the drain on a standard bathtub is in the correct spot for beneficial safety and comfort reasons and that most showers have it wrong.

First, the function of a shower is to get clean by washing away dirt with soap and water. Do you really want to stand in used soapy water while it drains —

More Involved Universal Design Solutions 63

sometimes slowly and hindered because you are standing on the drain? Your feet and ankles never get totally clean until you move away from the drain and rinse them again after most of the water completely drains.

Second, there is an uneven footing situation because of the way the floor slopes and pitches to the drain — from four different planes. This can be a slipping and balance issue. Many times, you will actually be standing right on the drain which is not particularly comfortable and hinders the function of the drain.

For anyone using a transfer bench or shower chair, it is very hard to position it easily and keep it in one place.

Third, you often have to move about to try to get away from the water that is pooling at the drain, and this can result in slippery footing and potentially a dangerous fall.

Finally, if you want to stand on something such as a shower mat, a teak platform, or nonslip treads, these do not conform well to the inverse pyramid design and must be adapted for use and to keep them from covering or blocking the drain.

The solution to this safety and comfort issue is to move the shower drain back to the front of the shower like it is in the tub.

For homes built on a crawl space or basement, moving the drain a couple of feet is not a huge issue but will likely take professionals to do it.

A slab foundation takes more work and more expense to break up part of the concrete and move the drain, but is worth it for the safety and comfort achieved.

The faucet, mixer, and shower head may be fine where they are. The drain is the main issue.

To allow water to drain faster and provide a sleeker look to the shower, a trench or linear drain is recommended.

The plumbing below the drain remains the same with just the way the water is collected on the surface changing. There are even surface drains that look much like the flush deco-drains used on pool decks that come in a variety of finishes, colors, and patterns.

The trench or linear drain that is located at the end of the shower ("forward"), with a flat shower floor gently pitched toward the drain, offers efficient draining and greater footing stability, accommodates the use of chairs or benches in the showers, and allows application of nonslip floor treatments.

Also, if someone else needs to be in the shower to offer assistance to a child or adult, it is easier for them to stand and move about on a flat service and one without the water pooling in the center.

It will take a little demolition and the work of a cement mason, a tile setter, a plumber, a handyman, kitchen and bath designer, or a remodeler to accomplish this drain makeover unless you are very skilled and confident in tackling a job such as this.

Zero-Step/No-Threshold/Barrier-Free Showers

When there is just a shower present with no bathtub, changing out the lip, threshold, transition, or step-up at the shower entrance to allow level access between the bathroom floor and the shower floor eliminates possible slipping or range-of-motion, balance, and coordination issues as someone steps from one surface to another — entering or leaving the shower — and allows free access to the shower by anyone.

It may look a little different than traditional showers that have a lip, step up, or raised shower pan, but this "zero-step" shower entrance is becoming more popular and eliminates many of the safety and access concerns normally present.

This project can be done at the same time as the floor drain relocation and shower floor modification. It will take a little demolition and the work of a cement mason, a tile setter, a plumber, a handyman, or a remodeler to accomplish unless you are very skilled at tackling a job such as this in your own home.

Shower Glass/Shower Doors

To keep as much water inside the tub or shower as possible while taking a shower or using the handheld shower, some bathtubs and showers have shower doors installed.

Generally, a single hinged door is used for a walk-in or stall shower, and a two- or three-panel bypass set of doors is used for a tub.

The tub doors are mounted in a track that covers the bath opening and slide inside and along a top and bottom track to keep water from splashing outside the tub or shower and onto the bathroom floor.

The lower track is held in place with adhesive caulk and the weight of the two or three doors. The side tracks are fastened to the walls or sides of the bath/shower area with screws or wall fasteners. The top track simply rests in place atop the two sides and has the weight of the doors keeping it in place.

Just adding the extra height and width of the lower track is enough to create a potential tripping hazard or entrance barrier for those people with balance or coordination issues, those with relatively short legs, and those with range-of-motion issues in the hips, ankles, or knees.

One-piece shower doors for stall showers typically open out into the room and generally have magnetic or ball closures that open rather easily and allow most anyone to use them.

However, they can easily release and pop open when fallen against or used for support during a slip — increasing the likelihood of a more serious fall and injury.

If they have a locking mechanism strong enough to prevent opening with incidental or light contact, they can create a safety hazard of a different nature and not be suitable for use by those not strong enough to operate the door.

They also can impact the area of approach and clearance around the shower as sufficient space needs to be allowed for people to open the door freely — and for the doors left or moved into in the open position not to obstruct access to anything else in the bathroom.

Outside of the issue of maintaining the glass or plexiglas panels to keep soap scum and mildew from forming or building up on the surface, there are other safety concerns and issues with the bypass doors and even the clear glass panels that are often used as walls or dividers along with shower doors to define the wet space and prevent water from getting into the rest of the room when the shower is used.

The soap or other build-up on the surface can make the surfaces slippery when touched or leaned against — from incidental contact to being used to try to keep from falling after a slip or loss of balance.

Depending on how they are installed and the type of glass used, the panels may not be able to support someone's weight or withstand a fall into it in a panic situation such as loss of balance, a slip, or fall.

If these glass panels were to break, flex, or dislodge from their mounts or supports, a more serious accident than just a fall could result.

Additionally, the glass doors and glass panels can reflect and refract light in a way that creates glare and affects orientation, depth perception, or the ability to tell where objects are.

Many of them also have towel bars attached which — in a panic situation — are used as grab bars and may break, pull loose, or cause the doors to come out of their tracks or otherwise fail to offer the support required.

In general, there are so many reasons of a safety, convenience, comfort, and accessibility nature for not using glass around a shower or bath area and not that many good ones that support their use.

It will take a little demolition and the work of a handyman, kitchen and bath designer, or a remodeler to accomplish removing the glass doors and panels unless you are a very skilled homeowner in tackling a job such as this. The glass panels or doors will be awkward and may be heavy. They could have sharp edges.

Also, they will need to be disposed of in some way.

Wet Room/Shower Room

If you have a relatively small bathroom, or you are working with one, creating a zero-step shower entrance presents additional challenges for keeping the rest of the room from getting wet when the shower is used.

One solution for this is to make the whole bathroom a wet room or shower room so that the entire space is capable of being wet.

This further eliminates the need to consider adding or retaining glass partitions, shower doors, and shower curtains.

It also allows the wet area of the shower (with one or more fixed showerheads or a handheld/personal shower) to be as large as necessary in the room without specifically defined boundaries. This also facilitates using it effectively, regardless of age and ability.

Because all of the walls and floor are tiled, any water from the shower will drain to the central floor drain.

The drain can be located under the showerhead or linearly (as mentioned on pages 62-65) from wall-to-wall (and parallel to the room's entrance door) along the general edge of the shower area. The floor would need to be pitched correctly for proper drainage.

Essentially, with this concept the bath is designed in such a way that most anything in it can get or be wet.

Just make sure to locate the toilet paper holder, towel bars, and cabinetry away from direct water contact or spray or bounce as much as possible — or that they can withstand a little water without damage.

Pedestal sinks or wall mounted sinks may do well in such an application to save space and eliminate the need for cabinets. Tankless and corner toilets can save some space also, but the soil pipe may need to be relocated.

Pocket doors or sliding doors, as already mentioned on page 56-57, may maximize the interior space without adding a door physically opening into the space — or out into the hallway.

Bath Temperature Setting/Scald Control

One way to avoid accidentally using water that is uncomfortably or dangerously hot in the bath or shower — and risking possible injury — is by setting the hot water heater to a maximum temperature of 120°.

Most dishwashers and washing machines have the heating ability within them to create the temperature above this that they need to perform properly. So, a lower hot water temperature may be the solution.

Still, many people may prefer a hotter temperature for a shower or for washing dishes by hand.

The safety and comfort solution here — and one regardless of ability or needs — is a temperature or scald control for the tub or shower. It can be set for the desired temperature to keep the water from getting any hotter than what is selected.

Depending on how handy you are as the homeowner or renter, you can do this yourself — or you can have a handyman, kitchen and bath designer, or remodeler do it for you.

Folding Shower Seats

Some people need to sit down routinely in order to use the shower and bathe comfortably and effectively. If this is the case, they should have a seat installed or integrated into the shower design.

However, as a component of universal design, a folding seat is a good strategy that offers safety, comfort, and convenience for everyone.

A seat that is out of the way except when needed serves everyone.

In households where the seat is required all the time by one or more people, you can leave it fully deployed, or one can be built in.

However, for people who require it occasionally, the folding seat can be opened into the operational position, used, and then stored again against the wall when they are finished.

Overnight or longer-term house guests can take advantage of it as well.

It can be designed in a variety of sizes and materials — as long as they are suitable for a wet area and can be cleaned easily.

Whether it's sitting to let the water massage a muscle pull or general muscles aches, sitting to keep stitches or surgical sites in the lower leg or foot from getting wet, sitting because of fatigue, sitting to shave your legs, or bathing small children or others who require assistance, a fold down seat accommodates a wide range of users and can be used when necessary and stored away when it isn't needed.

Because it needs to be anchored securely into the wall and ceramic tile or other hard surface surround materials are involved, homeowners or renters may want to have a remodeler, handyman, kitchen and bath designer, or durable medical equipment specialist do this job.

Handheld/Personal Showers

The handheld or personal shower is a great universal design strategy that offers safety, comfort, and convenience to all.

It can be an auxiliary shower to an existing fixed showerhead or the only showering device in a bathtub or stall shower.

It may be mounted along a slide bar, rest on a holder, or it might retract into the tub fixture.

When the handheld or personal shower is mounted along a slide bar where the height of it can be adjusted up or down along the length of the bar, some people may choose to leave it in place and just use it as a wall-mounted shower.

Others will remove the shower head from the mount and hold it.

When a folding or stationary shower seat is used, the handheld shower — with sufficient hose length — can easily be used by someone while they remain seated.

For bathing children or when other bathing assistance is required — or when a particular skin area needs to remain dry — the handheld offers good flexibility.

The main safety concern with a handheld is the way it is mounted for storage on the wall. There are slide bars that are being manufactured as grab bars — even with small diameters — and these are great.

Make sure to look for such a slide bar with the ability to be used as a grab bar in an emergency because it will be used as such anyway — even if it's not designed or intended to be used that way — just because it is there.

In existing applications where a handheld shower already exists but with a non-grab bar designed slider or mount, change it out with one that is designed for this purpose — and with stronger screws or anchors — so it can withstand a panic grab or offer additional support when needed.

Also, be careful that the hose is not a tripping hazard.

Adding a handheld shower can be a relatively simple do-it-yourself project, but a handyman or remodeler can do it as well.

Towel Bars/Hooks/Rings

This is a major safety issue in bathrooms.

Just as slide bars for a handheld or personal shower are not designed to be used as grab bars unless specifically manufactured and installed for this purpose — in addition to their slider function — towel bars generally are not designed for this purpose either.

Nevertheless, many towel bars and rings — especially those installed near or inside the tub or shower space — are used as a grab bar in a panic.

When someone loses their balance and slips, they look for the first thing they can find to support their weight or break their fall. The towel bar looks like it will work.

Unfortunately, many towel bars will break when sufficient downward or gripping pressure is applied to them — such as during a panic fall — or they may pull lose from the wall.

They are only designed to support a few towels and not someone's full body weight as they are falling. Even if the bars or rings don't actually break from the added pressure of someone trying to use them for support, they easily can pull lose from the wall. Either way, they will fail to support someone.

Nevertheless, there are towel bars designed to be used as grab bars also.

The important safety consideration is that when a towel is on the bar or rod, someone may grab it rather than the bar and it may slip off the bar and defeat the intended purpose.

For overall safety, comfort and convenience, towel bars should be mounted away from the actual shower or bath area so that they are not mistakenly used for support.

Hooks for towels do not tend to keep the towels on them very well and can cause injury if someone falls against them — or slips or trips on the towel that has fallen to the floor.

Changing out towel bars or moving them generally can be handled by the homeowner or renter unless you don't feel comfortable undertaking a job such as this or it's part of a more comprehensive remodeling project that you are undertaking.

Remember that they need to be anchored well into the wall in order to be effective.

Strategic Grab Bars

People tend to associate grab bars in a residential setting with people requiring them due to age or a specific need.

However, they do serve a useful universal design function when used as a positive strategy.

I call this concept "strategic grab bars" because I think for safety, comfort, and convenience, a well-designed, well-located, and attractive grab bar should be positioned vertically near the entrance to every tub or shower — at a suitable height for use by everyone in the household.

I think that everyone at least once in their lifetime has needed a little extra support getting in or out of the tub or shower.

This could be because they slipped or lost their balance getting in or out of the tub or shower. Perhaps they had an injury or recent surgery that kept them from putting their full weight on the ground, or they got a muscle cramp or spasm (in their leg, foot, or back) that interfered with their ability to stand or put their entire weight on their feet.

Maybe they were generally sore from exercise or other activity.

So, a strategic grab bar (probably just one per application) is a good universal design feature that can be incorporated into an aesthetically pleasing look.

Look for and replace all "pseudo-grab bars" with something that is specifically designed to provide the required support. Towel bars, soap dishes, toothbrush holders, or anything similar in the bath or shower area that might be grabbed by someone in a panic situation just are not designed to provide such support.

This would also include removing any grab bars mounted with suction cups. They simply cannot be relied upon to work when needed.

Grab bars must be designed to hold up to the pressure and force applied to them, and they must remain anchored to the wall.

Because of the safety factor involved here, you want to make sure that all grab bars are installed properly, so a handyman, kitchen and bath designer, or remodeler may be the appropriate one to do it.

Tilt-Out/Tip-Out Sink Front Bins

In the kitchen and baths, an area that goes unused that can be a great universal design strategy is the cabinet blank in front of the sink — one or two depending on the design, and with or without dummy drawer pulls.

For convenience and efficiency, these can be turned into functioning tilt-out or tip-out storage bins or trays — depending on their depth. Otherwise, they remain unused storage potential.

These can be used in the kitchen and bath and will replace medicine cabinets in bathrooms. They bring handy, everyday items right to your fingertips.

People of any age or ability can use these as they require very little effort to pull them down, don't latch but stay in place with tension hinges, and don't have a particularly large capacity so weight is usually not a concern.

The main safety concern would be keeping sharp items, medicines, and other dangerous items from such bins if there are young people living in the home or visiting the home.

Depending on how complicated it is to get the blank cabinet fronts off and replace them with the bins, this could easily be a do-it-yourself project.

Certainly a handyman or remodeler could do it.

If you are replacing cabinets, look for ones where this can be done.

There may not be enough room to employ this technique with undermount or integrated bowl sinks so check for available space first between the cabinet and the edge of the sink bowl.

Body Dryer

This is as high-tech, modern, and state-of-the-art as they come but very efficient and a great universal design strategy.

It provides safety, comfort, convenience, and is highly accessible.

This is a heated, forced air, electric dryer for use after showering.

It is mounted in a corner of the shower and provides a series of heated air jets to blow dry anyone in front of it much the same way that hair dryers or automatic hand dryers do.

They are said to take about the same amount of time that a person uses to towel dry, but towel drying does not remove all of the water like these do.

For anyone with range-of-motion issues, someone who might need help drying themselves, or anyone who needs to make sure they get completely dry, this is a great idea.

It can be used standing or seated.

It's a great conversation starter as well when guests or friends see it. Plus, it is quite sanitary and saves on laundering towels.

This is specifically designed for use in a wet area and is hardwired into the electrical circuit. You may need an electrician, handyman, or remodeler to install it.

Toe-Kick Lighting

The toe kick — that little recess of a few inches tall by a few inches deep that keeps the base cabinets from resting directly on the floor and gives people a place to put their feet to maintain one's balance while in front of the cabinets — can be put to effective use with LED rope lighting, fluorescent strip lighting, xenon strip lighting, or LED strip lighting.

This provides additional indirect ambient lighting for the kitchen, bath, or laundry room — for safety or general illumination in an otherwise unused space.

It can be installed with a dimmer control if desired. It also can be switched, used with a timer or photo cell, or just left on because of its energy efficiency.

Depending on what type of lighting is selected and where the electrical outlet or electricity source happens to be, this might be as simple as plug-it-in-and-use it.

It might be an installation that you can do, or it might require the services of an electrician or low voltage electrical contractor (also called an electrical services contractor).

It makes a great night light and helps out in low-light situations when overhead or other lights are not on or available. It is inexpensive to use since it uses very little energy.

Under-Cabinet/Task Lighting

The kitchen requires a variety of lighting sources since there are so many different types of tasks going on there.

Another underutilized area of the kitchen (and the bath and laundry room) for additional lighting is the area under the upper cabinets.

As is the case for toe-kick lighting, adding lighting there might be a simple plug-in-and-use installation that you can do or require the services of an electrician or low voltage electrical contractor or electrical services contractor — depending on where the electrical outlet or electricity source happens to be and if a new connection or outlet has to be installed.

This could also be part of a larger kitchen (or bath) remodeling project.

This provides additional countertop, workspace, and indirect ambient lighting for the kitchen or bath.

It can be switched, used with a timer, or just left on because of its energy efficiency — LED rope lighting, fluorescent strip lighting, xenon strip lighting, or LED strip lighting.

This is a solution that provides additional safety and convenience by adding more light to the countertop work and prep surface and to the room in general.

It also makes a great night light and helps out in low-light situations when overhead or other lights are not switched on.

Overhead Lighting

At one time, homes were built with ceiling light fixtures in every room. While they often delivered harsh, localized lighting that could cast strong shadows and didn't fill the entire room with effective lighting, each room at least had this light source.

For older homes where this is still true (where they haven't been removed or replaced with an updated fixture) and for newer homes where foyers, living rooms, dining rooms, bedrooms, kitchens, baths, hallways, stairways, laundry rooms, porches, patios, garages, and basements may have ceiling light fixtures also, the light output is often insufficient for the activity in the room or space — making this a safety, convenience, and comfort issue.

Depending on the size, shape, and design of the lighting fixtures and the number and wattage of bulbs they can support, it may be possible to increase the light output.

Be aware of shadows and glare caused by overhead lights that may affect vision and depth perception and be a comfort and safety concern.

In some cases, increasing the bulb wattage may be sufficient, while in other instances a new or additional light fixture may be required as the solution.

The type of light bulbs available for consumers to use in ceiling fixtures has changed. Incandescent bulbs have been phased out. The CFL's (compact florescent bulbs) have safety, health, and practical concerns (sometimes they don't fit well or are unattractive) involved with using them.

Regular florescent tubes and rings (with less safety and health issues than CFL's but still some present) and halogen bulbs (although they produce a lot of heat) can still be used.

LED lighting is the trend of the future.

They tend to cost more initially but last several years, can be used with a dimmer, are being manufactured in higher wattage outputs, and are more widely available than they were.

To supplement overhead lighting, you can use table lamps and floor lamps in bedrooms, living rooms, dining rooms, home offices, basements, porches, family rooms, and other living areas — again paying attention to the light output, shadows, glare, and "hot spots."

Remember to increase the wattage as necessary and feasible for safety, convenience, and comfort.

In living rooms, dining rooms, family rooms, bathrooms, and bedrooms, wall lamps or sconces offer supplemental lighting but generally not enough to light a large area.

In kitchens and bathrooms, the toe-kick and under-cabinet or task lighting that I mentioned are great supplemental lighting sources.

While consumers can change out light bulbs rather easily, you may or may not feel confident in replacing light fixtures and choose to rely on the services of a handyman, electrician, or remodeler. This would be especially true if a new receptacle, wall switch, or circuit needs to be installed or the fixture is particularly large or heavy.

Many ceiling fans come with light kits optional or already installed. This provides a central ceiling light resource also — with the same issues as ceiling mounted fixtures in terms of light output, harsh light, glare, and shadows.

Ceiling Fans

Ceiling fans are great for providing comfort and air circulation. As I just mentioned, they can also function as ceiling light fixtures.

They can supplement other ceiling or wall-mounted light fixtures that might be present in the room and can provide a central light (with one or more bulbs mounted in the center of the fan under the blade motor) or an array of several bulbs extending from the center. They come in a variety of styles and shapes also.

Keeping lights and fans dusted (air quality and general appearance) and avoiding a strobing effect (with the fan creating a pulsing light pattern on the walls, ceiling, or floors) are the main issues with ceiling fans and the lights attached to them.

For additional comfort and convenience, the fans can be regulated for speed (as well as downdraft or updraft), and the lights that are attached to them can be used with a dimmer control.

Some homeowners or tenants can install their own ceiling fans as long as they have the physical ability to lift it into position, hold it in place while the wiring is connected, and attach it to the mounting hook.

Otherwise, a handyman, electrician, carpenter, or remodeler can do this.

Skylights

Continuing the discussion of lighting in your home for comfort, safety, and convenience, let's look at skylights. In any room where additional overhead lighting is desired — primarily during daylight hours — skylights are a good choice.

As long as they are installed properly so that there are no leaks and are not shadowed excessively by overhanging tree branches (an occasional branch blowing in the breeze may be OK), skylights (when ceiling space and rafters accommodate or allow their use) can be an effective lighting source.

Also, they will reduce the energy demand for other lighting during daylight hours so there is an economic benefit as well.

Depending on how the rafters are configured relative to the ceiling in a particular room, the skylights may not be able to be as large as desired or centered in the room — aesthetics may be a factor in ultimately deciding on whether to use them in a specific room.

Skylights come in square and rectangular shapes with either flat or domed lenses — fixed and well as being able to open and close.

They also come round with polished steel tubes connecting a ceiling lens or diffuser with the roof lens (available in a variety of diameters and from various manufacturers).

The round skylights also have light kits so that they can double as a ceiling light during evening hours or other times with supplemental room lighting is needed.

This project definitely will require the services of a remodeler, carpenter, handyman, roofer, or skylight installer — and possibly an interior designer, architect, and electrician (for the light kit) — to make sure the skylights are located correctly, the roof and ceiling are cut in the right place, the alignment is made with the ceiling location, everything is trimmed out properly, and that there are no leaks.

Eye-Level Controls

This is a universal design element that addresses accessibility, comfort, convenience, and safety issues in your home.

Often the wall-mounted controls in a home, such as thermostats and switches for ceiling fans (and even some light switches) are mounted higher than eye level (making them hard to see and use easily) or beyond the easy reach of a child, short adult, or person in a wheelchair. However, regular light switches typically are located at a reasonable height.

Controls that are located generally less than 48" (4 feet) above the floor allow the widest range of accessibility and usage.

Thus, the small child or adult, those who might be in a wheelchair, those who might have physical limitations that keep them from standing erect (including those requiring support from a cane or walker), those with range-of-motion issues in their elbows or shoulders that prevent a normal arm extension could reach them — in addition to those of average or above average height.

Sometimes mixing or distribution valves in tubs and showers as well as the digital displays and controls for wall ovens and microwaves fall into this same category of being mounted higher than easily accessible or visible in terms of being able to read them and set them correctly.

Eye level for a typical adult in a wheelchair is defined by the ADA as 51" — a smaller or larger person could experience a little variation in this number.

Still, other national standards (such as the Uniform Federal Accessibility Standards — "UFAS") call for controls to be no higher than 54" from the floor for a person in a wheelchair to reach if they are alongside and directly beneath it and no higher than 48" from the floor for them to reach if they are in front of and facing it.

This might be somewhat dependent on the length of someone's arm, but it seems to be a reasonable height for children and smaller adults also. Of course "no higher than" means they can be lower.

If wall controls are placed in the general vicinity of light switches, they would be more convenient and aesthetically pleasing than having them take up more wall space and not be as centrally located.

In terms of safety and comfort, it's beneficial for more rather than fewer people in the home to be able to access and use these controls — including being able to read them and set them (the adjustable or programmable ones such as the thermostats I discussed on pages 41-43) because they are at a comfortable height.

If the wiring going to the controllers or devices is long enough to allow relocating or moving them without any rewiring, this could be a do-it-yourself project for you. Of course, the walls would need to be patched and repainted where the former installations were.

An electrician, handyman, or remodeler may need to do this work — especially if there is not enough wire going to the controller or switch to allow it to be moved without running more wiring or you don't feel comfortable with working around electrical wires.

Electrical Outlets

Depending on the building codes in effect where you are, the standard location of an electrical outlet from the floor is likely fine.

However, installing standard electrical receptacles higher than usual above the floor so they are in easy reach of everyone is a good universal design strategy as long as they are not so high as to call attention to their placement.

In some rooms such as kitchens, bathrooms, and laundry rooms, the outlets tend to be higher anyway — just over the height of countertops or adjacent to them.

Sometimes, they are mounted in the sides of the base cabinets if they are accessible in the room.

In other rooms such as bedrooms, outlets can be a little higher because furniture often hides them and makes them difficult to access when installed closer to the floor.

The height from the floor that outlets normally are placed is not inconsistent with the UFAS guidelines (9" for direct access by a person in a wheelchair and 18" for someone reaching for it from a wheelchair position), but if they were installed a little higher, more people could reach them easier without bending so much.

This would include taller adults, people using a walker, people with range-of-motion issues, and those who have difficulty bending down or standing up again.

Depending on how many outlets need to be moved and how sufficient the wiring is going to the various outlets, this could be a do-it-yourself project. The walls would need to be patched and repainted where the former boxes were.

An electrician, handyman, or remodeler may need to do this work — especially when there is not enough wiring to move the boxes without running more wiring.

Wall-Mounted Mirrors

All homes need mirrors, and they are generally found in bathrooms, bedrooms and foyers or hallways.

Many are decorative mirrors — regardless of size or shape — that are framed and hung on the wall like a picture.

Some, such as in bathrooms, are large and mounted directly to the wall with adhesive or clips.

Others are considered to be "full-length" and attach to the back of a door.

Still others are used as bypass or bi-fold closet door panels.

The way that mirrors become a universal design concept and strategy is when they are accessible and usable by everyone in the home.

They don't necessarily have to be a tilted mirror that adjusts on a pivot (aiming somewhat downward with the top of the mirror being further from the wall that the bottom), but this can be a universal design treatment if everyone in the home can use the mirror comfortably and see themselves in it.

Generally, the height at which tilt or fixed mirrors are mounted and the focal length created by the installation (particularly with a tilted mirror) means that the mirrors are too high to see more than just your head and upper torso.

Mirrors mounted behind the sink are no lower than 30" unless the countertop is lower. Often mirrors are higher than this because of a clearance space allowed between the countertop and the bottom of the mirror.

Additionally, there usually there is a wall opposite the wall-mounted mirror that keeps someone from backing up far enough to get a longer view.

Even when you get a full body view from a wall-mounted mirror, the distance is such that you are quite far from the mirror. Then, being able to see much detail for grooming or choosing an outfit becomes an issue.

Lighting above or around the mirrors further affects the functionality of the mirrors due to glare, "hot spots," insufficient lighting, shadows, and the color temperature of the bulbs.

Full-length and closet door panels offer a much better solution than wall-mounted mirrors because they accommodate any physical size. A toddler, a person in a wheel chair, and a basketball player can all see themselves in such mirrors. You can get as close as necessary to the mirror.

In selecting mirrors, pay attention to the weight of the mirrors relative to where they will be installed or used, the likelihood of the mirrors beginning to de-silver along the edges, and the general quality of the glass so imperfections are avoided. Nevertheless, mirrors are relatively inexpensive to purchase.

Some homeowners and renters can handle a project of this nature, but a professional can do this easily.

Visual Indicators

I have already talked about visual clues to indicate relative temperatures and show where light switches and other controls are located.

There are other visual indicators that are universal design concepts that are effective.

For the hearing impaired, doorbells and telephones are often connected to one or more lights throughout the home that flash when someone rings the doorbell or calls on the phone.

They might be in the living room, kitchen, bedroom, or other areas of the home.

They are a great feature for anyone (and thus universal in concept) because they provide another — and silent — way of alerting us to the presence of someone at the front door or on the phone (for those people who have a landline).

With all of the noise present in a home from time-to-time — from TVs, music players, computer videos, conversation, appliances, vacuum cleaners, fans, and other devices — having a visual way of knowing when someone is at the door or calling on the phone would help everyone. There are outside noises present at various times also.

Small children could easily see and recognize the visual signal, as could anyone else in the home.

This is a feature that offers safety, comfort, and convenience to the home and its occupants.

There are some easy-to-install kits that can be obtained from electronic stores for you to install yourself.

Otherwise, an electrician, handyman, ESC (low-voltage electrical services contractor), or remodeler can do this job for you.

5

Other Universal Design Strategies

Additional Strategies For Safety, Convenience, Comfort And Accessibility

There are several other universal design strategies, treatments, and recommendations that we should look at that positively impact the overall quality of life in your home.

The following design concepts and solutions can be used in an existing home such as yours when included as part of a more comprehensive remodeling than just changing out a few fixtures or moving the location of various controls.

They also can be added into a new home about to be built or one in the early stages of construction where such changes are still possible.

The objective with such design considerations is increasing the comfort, safety, convenience, and accessibility.

Some of these concepts are going to have wider appeal than others, but all can be effective — and all are universal.

These strategies will require some advance planning and consultation. In some cases, major changes are involved.

The issue is not whether they apply to all ages and abilities but whether you want to incorporate them in any renovation projects that you are doing or planning.

Contrast And Glare

As we age, our eyes are more affected by bright lights and glare. We are more susceptible to misjudging distances and determining how close objects are that might be in front of us.

Some people have more pronounced vision issues than others — regardless of age.

Therefore, two strategies that are effective for eliminating glare or confusion about surfaces and where objects are located are the use of color or contrast and using less shiny or reflective surfaces.

Other Universal Design Strategies

Glass (window glass, mirrors, glass panels in appliances, and glass shower enclosures — if you haven't removed them yet) and hard surfaces such as countertops, appliance fronts (unless they have a matte finish), and ceramic and polished hardwood flooring are especially prone to reflecting light sources and creating glare when overhead lights are used. Sometimes natural light can do this also.

In kitchens, often a monochromatic look is used to be aesthetically pleasing, but it is not the best design for universal accessibility, safety, and comfortable use.

It needs to be obvious where countertops and floors are located and not just blend from one surface to another.

A technique for defining countertops is something called "edge-banding" where a contrasting color is used on the edge of the countertops to show where the countertop surface begins.

Doing this with some hard surfaces such as granite or quartz will take more effort and will add to the cost. However, it will make the kitchen safer.

As for the flooring, toe-kick lighting that I already mentioned will illuminate part of the floor to show its location relative to the cabinets and reduce glare as well.

Using red knobs on stove or cooktop fronts is a similar strategy, as is another that I already mentioned – adding a device to the end of faucets (when it will fit) that lights up blue for cold water and red for hot or using a faucet that displays a color for the relative temperature setting.

Flooring

Flooring is a matter of personal choice, but there are types of flooring that tend to be more problematic than others for air quality, maintenance, accessibility, comfort, and safety.

Thus, there are universal design choices and strategies concerning flooring.

In general, carpet is not a good choice anywhere in the home.

When carpeting gets wet from rain or snow being tracked onto it or from outerwear, shoes, or umbrellas dripping onto it – or when the door is opened and the wind blows in the rain or snow – it tends to remain wet for a period of time. Pets will track in the precipitation and dirt also.

Wet carpeting is more susceptible to attracting dirt, leaving noticeable dirty marks or stains that remain even after the area is dry.

Carpeting shows stains from food (especially ones with sauces, condiments, and gravies) and beverage spills (wine, fruit juice, Kool-Aid, coffee, tea, milk). It stains from pet accidents, blood from cuts, and anything else tracked or spilled onto it (oil, grease, mud).

Carpeting tends to off-gas, and it retains dirt and other pet and airborne allergens. More than other types of flooring, it develops noticeable wear patterns.

It presents air quality issues and typically needs replacing every few years. It also fades from the UV rays in sunlight and florescent lighting.

Carpeting needs constant vacuuming or shampooing and is never really showroom clean again. Small, sometimes sharp objects can fall into the carpet and be unnoticeable until stepped on.

While aesthetically beneficial, area rugs are similar to carpeting and can be a slipping or tripping hazard — particularly when used in doorways between rooms or in the kitchen or bathroom in front of the sink. Nearly everyone is susceptible to this danger.

Like carpeting, area rugs hold dirt and allergens, but they generally can be laundered more frequently.

To maintain true universal design, the use of area rugs and carpeting in the home would be disallowed for safety, air quality, maintenance, general comfort, and accessibility.

Hard surface flooring is the best to use, but hardwood flooring or hardwood-like flooring (engineered wood, laminates, and bamboo) should not be used in wet areas. Moisture causes the grain to expand and contract and affects the seams and joints.

Laminates and engineered wood flooring do not breathe so any water spilled on them will be trapped beneath them when it seeps through the joints and seams.

Bamboo is water resistant (not waterproof), but it is not recommended for use in areas where it could get wet.

Ceramic tile — especially the new reticulated tile that fits together tightly and requires very small to even no grout lines — is a hard surface that holds up well to water, spills, and foot traffic.

It is available in a variety of sizes and colors to match the color palette of the room in which it is installed and fit the proportions of the room.

The main issue with ceramic flooring is safety — being slick or slippery when wet or too shiny which creates glare (as I already mentioned) or prohibits good traction for walking across safely or using an aid such as a cane or walker.

In these cases, treads of some type or a smaller tile or mosaic pattern that is inlaid in places will provide more traction.

Ceramic tile typically shows wear patterns less than other types of flooring.

Vinyl flooring has made a comeback.

It generally is well accepted and comes in a variety of patterns and colors. It offers a little cushion so it is easier on the feet and legs when standing on it and comes in several sizes and installation options.

Another type of flooring material that seems to work well — especially in the kitchen — is the natural product cork.

Cork is especially nice to stand on and helps to cushion dishes and glasses when they are accidentally dropped onto it.

Some homeowners will be able to accomplish flooring removal and replacement, but most will rely on handymen, flooring contractors, tile setters, or remodelers. It also depends on what is being removed as far as dust and debris.

There also is the issue of disposing of the removed product.

If you are removing tile that has been in place for years, approach it cautiously. It could have asbestos in the tile or in the mastic used to adhere it to the floor.

If you suspect this is the case or you are unsure, have it evaluated before proceeding.

Automatic Dustpan

Keeping hard surface floors clean requires constant attention. Vacuuming or sweeping with a broom are daily activities to keep the floors presentable.

There are vacuums, electric brooms, and other devices that can be used, but they tend to be a little bulky, can be hard for some people to move them about, and generally require electricity to use them.

There are manual mops, brooms, and sweepers, but a device that is universal that may have application for you is the automatic dustpan.

A central vacuum system is required for this feature to work so a remodeling contractor or a central vacuum installer may be needed to accomplish this design.

You also need the space to install it.

Do-it-yourselfers can complete this project, depending on how easy it is to gain access to the walls and attic or basement and how much disruption in the home can be tolerated while it is being installed. Some drywall repair and painting likely will be required.

A central vacuum system is a great idea to have in the home, but it is not purely a universal design feature.

It offers convenience as far as being able to plug the hose into various wall ports located around the home instead of moving an upright or canister vacuum cleaner around the house, but it still requires some physical size, strength, range-of-motion, stamina, and coordination to be able to use it effectively.

The automatic dustpan port is a station connected to the central vacuum that is installed at floor level in the baseboard (available in various finished and colors).

It is activated by a foot switch.

Simply sweep the floor and move the dust pile to the automatic dustpan where it can be vacuumed away into the holding tank.

This is a universal design feature because anyone capable of using a broom — even from a wheelchair or while using a walker — can sweep a pile of dust toward the automatic dustpan.

The switch on the port can be activated without bending down. Just step on it or use the broom handle or similar object to activate it.

This also is another way to improve indoor air quality by making it easier to remove dust from the floors.

Room-To-Room Transitions

When two different types or thicknesses of flooring meet in a doorway — or between rooms even without a doorway — an uneven transition between the two surface results, and it can present comfort, safety, and accessibility issues.

Even using a molding strip (metal, wood, rubber, or vinyl) between the two surfaces, going from one surface height (regardless of what it is) to another can present challenges for kids pushing toys along the floor, baby strollers, walkers, wheelchairs, and even furniture or carts on casters.

Walking from one surface to the other can even be a potential tripping or stumbling hazard for anyone who catches the heel of their shoe or their toe (wearing shoes or not) on the molding.

A uniform thickness of flooring — even if it's not the same product throughout the home — is the safe and comfortable way to handle this issue.

Depending on the number of instances where this exists in your home, it might be a do-it-yourself project to remedy the affected areas.

More than likely, this type of project will need to be done by a remodeler or flooring contractor.

Of course, replacing or redoing the flooring in most or all of your home will eliminate this issue. This would be a great opportunity to eliminate carpeting and solve the additional issue of uneven transitions at the same time.

Motorized Shelving

Sometimes the height differential between members in a home is so great that solutions are sought for accommodating the location of shelving or countertops in closets, kitchens, and other areas where people can have access to them easily.

This is an optional solution — not for everyone and not for every budget. However, it does provide the ability to accommodate a very wide range of individual users in a single household.

When people in a household have differing needs — because they range from tall to short, some are using assistance such as a wheelchair, some just prefer to sit when preparing meals or need to because of stamina or balance issues, or some prefer countertops and other surfaces at a lower or higher height than "normal" — motorized shelving has the ability to bring many things to a comfortable height (up or down from a typical height) for the person desiring to use whatever it is that can be adjusted this way.

This is a universal feature because it is designed for convenience and comfort as much as it is for safety and accessibility.

This can be used in a closet to move items around on a track — or up and down — in a tight space, or just for convenience.

It can be used in the bath or powder room to allow access to literally anyone of any height or ability by moving a sink (vessel or one mounted in a small countertop) up and down as long as the water supply lines and drain tubing are flexible and installed with this in mind.

It can be used in the kitchen to provide comfortable and accessible eating space by moving a countertop up or down. It also can be used to raise or lower cabinets, shelving, cooktops, and sinks.

A handyman, kitchen and bath designer, interior designer, remodeler, or electrician would be a good resource for accomplishing this — depending on the extent of the changes desired.

Only for someone very experienced in do-it-yourself electrical and mechanical projects might this be done by the owner or tenant.

Kitchen Islands

In homes where there is an island as a feature in the kitchen, a couple of safety, convenience, and access issues need to be addressed.

Most of the islands I have seen in new home designs and in doing kitchen assessments in existing homes are too large for the kitchen floor space.

People like the idea of having an island, but quite often there simply is not enough space around the island for two people to be in the same area at the same time or for a cabinet or appliance door to open easily.

Sometimes it's difficult for even one person to navigate the space around the island.

There needs to sufficient clear space — generally 48"-60" — around each of the three or four sides of the island where cabinets, appliances, tables, passageways, or other functional areas of the kitchen are located.

It's not just a matter of someone in a wheelchair being able to move around the island easily. This is a matter of general access and function as well as comfort, convenience, and safety.

While wheelchair access is a consideration, it's a larger issue of two or more people — comfortably and safely — being able to be in the kitchen at the same time without bumping into each other, blocking the passageway, or interfering with what the other one is doing.

This would be true whether they are standing or seated.

Sometimes when the islands are really large for the kitchen space, it's tight for even one person to be in the kitchen and move around comfortably.

Thus, opening cabinet doors and drawers, using the oven or cooktop, opening the dishwasher, opening and using the microwave, preparing food, accessing the sink, and opening the refrigerator (or getting water or ice from the in-door dispenser) are actions that could go on simultaneously — or nearly so — with two or more people in the kitchen together.

People might not even be in the kitchen together for the same reason.

For instance, one person (or even more than one) might be eating or preparing a snack, getting a larger meal started, cleaning up from an earlier meal, washing dishes in the sink, putting dishes or groceries away, getting something to drink from the refrigerator, getting out pots or pans for meal preparation, washing their hands, making or getting a cup of coffee, reading the paper, or using their computer or tablet on the countertop — and the other person or persons could be doing a different one of these activities or even something else.

Regardless of the size of the island — after it is adjusted to fall within acceptable clearance distances — all of the corners should be rounded with a radius sufficient to prevent injury from accidentally running into it while walking past or falling against it.

For universal design, if the resulting island is large enough for someone to sit down at it and eat — rather than just being a food preparation area or serving station — part of the countertop should be low enough and open enough to allow people to sit (or pull up a wheelchair) and eat.

In such cases, remember (as I mentioned on page 99) to mark the edges of the countertop to show that they are at different heights.

Restyling or resizing an island will likely involve the services of a handyman, kitchen and bath designer, interior designer, cabinet installer, remodeler, carpenter, electrician, or plumber — or several of them — depending on the extent of the changes needed.

A consumer experienced with do-it-yourself projects of this magnitude might be able to tackle this.

Modular Sink Base Cabinets

While having roll-in access to the kitchen or bathroom sinks is often desired, not everyone needs it. For this reason, it's not recommended as a universal design feature.

Nevertheless, as both a universal design and adaptable design feature, sink base cabinets in the kitchen and bathrooms can be designed and created intentionally to be removed later on as necessary — to create a more open look or to allow wheelchair access.

When the sink base cabinet is designed and created as a modular unit, it can be taken out (with those cabinets on either side of it remaining in place) to allow full access for someone in a wheelchair or just more open space for use with a chair or bench.

The removable, modular sink base cabinet would be a unit entirely separate from the rest of the cabinetry that can be installed along with the cabinets on either side of it but removed later without affecting the integrity of the remaining cabinets or countertop.

It is universal because it shows no outward sign of being any different from the other cabinets at present, but it is easily adaptable when the time comes for a fully accessible sink by simply removing the modular sink base unit.

Of course, there are other solutions for creating wheelchair access at the sink by removing the cabinet doors and cabinet floor or designing them to be retracted.

The height of the countertop also would need to be evaluated to make sure that it can be accessed effectively.

As I mentioned earlier, a wall hung sink or a pedestal sink would allow wheelchair access without any other design changes required.

If it's just installing modular cabinets and securing them, a homeowner experienced in this type of job might do it. For the countertop, plumbing, and other aspects of this project, a remodeler, carpenter, plumber, or kitchen and bath designer may be needed.

Retractable Sink Base Cabinet Doors

While a modular sink base cabinet can be installed to be removed at a later date to provide wheelchair access to a sink, a universal design solution rather than an adaptable one is to create retractable doors on the sink base cabinet.

To allow access whenever someone needs to roll up to the sink from a wheelchair — or use it from a seated position (for stamina or just convenience) — the doors on the cabinet can be created to retract on a track or groove along the inside walls of the cabinet much like the doors on a TV cabinet or entertainment center used to do.

It may not even be necessary to remove the toe-kick, but if that is desired, there are two way to handle this.

The toe-kick (the part of the cabinet floor extending from the door to the vertical toe-kick riser as well as the riser itself) for this base cabinet can be removed and left off so that when the doors are open and used in the retracted position, the place where the toe-kick normally would be is empty.

The cabinet floor also can be hinged and folded back inside the cabinet (with the toe kick riser either coming with the floor or remaining in place). If it moves with the cabinet flooring, the toe-kick can be moved out of the way when cabinet access is desired even if the doors are just opened and not retracted.

With this method, the outward appearance is the same whether or not the cabinet is designed for wheelchair access — instead of having a noticeable missing toe-kick.

Another solution is to remove the toe-kick and then to reconfigure the remaining cabinet floor.

It can be designed as an plumbing access panel (when access is needed or desired) on a slant to provide open floor space in front of it, conceal the plumbing behind it, and have narrow open shelves on it for storing cleaning products and paper goods.

The doors need to be kept from moving inward past the flush closed position when not retracted. A stop, pin, cleat, or other device needs to be used to achieve this.

A homeowner experienced in woodworking type projects might be able to do this; however, a remodeler, carpenter, cabinet installer, or kitchen and bath designer may be needed.

Cabinets And Drawers

Cabinets are a big focus of universal design because they are used in many rooms throughout the home, and storage is something everyone needs.

There are several universal design strategies involving upper and base cabinets — beyond what I already mentioned about the pulls, the tilt-out/tip-out bins, the toe-kick lighting, task lighting, and the modifications to the sink base cabinets.

Many of these opportunities can be do-it-yourself projects, but someone such as a remodeler, handyman, carpenter, kitchen and bath designer, interior designer, or architect can get involved also.

There really are two main issue concerning cabinets: accessibility and ease of use.

In designing cabinets for replacement or in reworking existing cabinets — in the kitchen, bathrooms, basement, laundry room, linen closet, bedroom closets, garage, summer kitchen, mud room, patio, home office, dining room, hallways, or wherever else they are located in the home, look at the size of the doors and drawers, the physical weight of the doors and drawers, the flexibility of using the storage space, the location of the door or drawer pulls on the actual doors or drawers, and the amount of room in front of them for someone to access them.

Ease of retrieving items that are stored is a big issue.

With drawers or pull-out shelves, bins, or baskets, the suspension system needs to provide sufficient support for the weight and easy movement of the drawers, shelves, bins, or baskets in and out — whether they are empty or loaded to capacity.

Other Universal Design Strategies 117

Thus, they should not be dependent on someone of any particular strength or ability being able to use them.

They should work equally well whether they are being accessed by someone from a standing, seated, or kneeling position.

To appeal to everyone in the household — regardless of their age, size, or ability — a good design idea for ultimate storage efficiency is to approach it much the same way that we want the controls to be located in the home.

You'll recall from page 90 that the guidelines are for them to be located 48"-54" or less from the floor.

Obviously, cabinets are taller than that and can go all the way to the ceiling, but they should be designed so that most of the commonly used items are easily accessible and retrievable at eye level or below.

Keeping the items most in demand and most frequently used at least one shelf up from the floor is part of this same strategy.

One strategy is to install upper cabinets actually resting on the countertop.

While this concept makes them more accessible, it takes away useable counterspace that must be accounted for and accommodated elsewhere in the room. An island — if the dimensions of the kitchen and intended size of the island permit it to be used — can be a solution.

An alternative is to mount one or more upper cabinets lower than their traditional height but still up from the countertop a few inches — making them easier to reach than at their traditional height and preserving some countertop functionality.

As I mentioned in discussing closet doors on page 61, another good idea is to look for smaller doors and cabinets so that a floor-to-ceiling linen, pantry, or supply cabinet can actually have two or more separate parts rather than a very tall closet-like cabinet — that comes with a necessarily heavier, larger, and harder-to-control door.

Some designers and consumers are returning to an open-look where just open wall shelves are used for storing cups, glasses, and dishware — in place of cabinets.

There may or may not be upper cabinets used in conjunction with this design.

The openness certainly enhances accessibility. Safety may be more of a concern as objects could fall or be knocked from the shelves.

Along this same line, open cabinets are being used that have no doors on them. Again, access is enhanced, but knocked items from the cabinet or having them fall out may present safety concerns.

Also, keeping the dishware and glasses dusted is necessary since there are no doors to protect them. Clutter is another potential issue with open shelves.

Depending your ability and expertise, you may be able to do some or all of the work on the cabinets; however, the services of someone such as a handyman, remodeler, carpenter, kitchen and bath designer, architect, interior designer, or occupational therapist may be beneficial for an effective design and proper installation.

Kitchen Desk

A sit-down desk that can be installed inline in a base cabinet run or separately along another wall in the kitchen — as a standalone or with other base cabinets and often with upper cabinets or shelving is a concept that many people already use.

Once marketed as a "recipe desk," it now serves as the more universal "kitchen desk."

This is a great universal design concept that has multiple uses for a variety of ages and abilities.

However, the kitchen area may need to be enlarged or reconfigured to allow the use of the kitchen desk.

The desk can be entirely open with just a countertop covering the space, or it can have a single desk drawer beneath the countertop or two or more adjacent drawers (depending on the width of the opening (knee space).

It can also have one or two of the drawer base cabinet units on either or both sides of the knee space much like a traditional desk.

The countertop can be the same height as the other countertop space in the kitchen, but it is more versatile at a lower height in the 30" range — or even at the 29" typical desktop height.

Since this is a fairly common feature in many kitchens, the design does not suggest anything unusual, and it fits right in.

Still, it allows wheelchair access as well as the ability for anyone else in the household (including kids doing their homework) to use this space.

It can be designed or used as a computer or TV/movie station (with a TV, desktop computer, notebook, or tablet) or just remain an open countertop for crafts, writing, meal planning, eating, meal or baking preparation (where doing it from a seated position is necessary or desired), cooking with a small appliance (coffee maker, crockpot, toaster oven, microwave, or induction burner) at a lower counter height, or several other uses where a desktop is beneficial because of its height, openness, and accessibility.

It can accommodate wheelchair access and be used without any adaptation.

Any small appliance can easily and safely be used on the countertop without taking up all of the available space.

Depending on the size of the job, you can purchase the cabinets and countertops from the home center store and install them yourself.

Otherwise, the services of a remodeler, carpenter, handyman, kitchen and bath designer, or interior designer will be required.

Sit-Down Vanity

This is similar in design and concept to the kitchen desk and has been used in the master bathrooms of many homes for years.

It has never gone out of style, but its popularity seems to rise and fall in new construction of production homes.

Like the kitchen desk, the sit-down vanity can be installed inline in a vanity base cabinet run or separately along another wall in the bath — as a standalone.

Also like the kitchen desk, the sit-down vanity can be entirely open with just a countertop covering the space, or it can have one or more desk drawers immediately under the countertop (depending on the width of the opening — knee space).

It can even be built to look like a desk with vertical drawer units installed along one or both sides of the knee space.

As a universal design feature, the sit-down vanity, which is typically installed in the master bathroom (or occasionally in a dressing area near the bath), can also be used in the guest or secondary bathrooms for children or guests to use for their grooming needs.

A typical desktop height is 29" and many bathroom vanities are built to this height. They range all the way to 36". Some people like the sit-down portion of the vanity to be at the same height as the rest of the bathroom base cabinets, while others prefer it to be slightly to definitely lower.

While the height of the sit-down vanity can vary, the concept of the sit-down portion itself is a nice universal design feature that is widely used.

Again, depending on the size and complexity of the project, you may desire to purchase the cabinets and countertops from the home center store and install them.

Otherwise, the services of a remodeler, carpenter, handyman, kitchen and bath designer, or interior designer will be required.

Up-Front Controls

To make washing machines, laundry sinks, ranges, garbage disposals, range hoods, exhaust fans, cooktops, microwaves, ovens, and other appliances and fixtures in the home as accessible and usable by as many people as possible, the operating controls, switches, handles, digital displays, and everything else connected with operating the appliances and fixtures need to be located on the top surface of the appliance or fixture (at the front edge) or preferably on or near the front of the appliance, fixture, or device.

Certain appliances already are created this way — the front-loading washing machine and induction cooktop, for instance.

Many appliances can be switched out for ones more accessible when it comes time to replace them, and you can do this or use a remodeler or handyman to do this.

Some of the changes will require moving or adding switches, and an electrician may need to get involved also.

Easy-Access Appliances

Kitchen and other major appliances are used in the home every day so we need to look at making them more accessible and useable by everyone in the household.

The appliances that come to mind that have great solutions already available are washing machines, refrigerators, cooktops, ranges, and dishwashers.

Others, such as ovens, clothes dryers, and microwaves, need to be selected or installed with universal design and accessibility in mind.

The front-loading washing machine has the controls and the door located on the front so that anyone can use it. It can even be raised with a pedestal base if it needs to be a little higher for members of the household.

A top loading washing machine does not provide these advantages.

Refrigerators come in two styles that offer great accessibility — the side-by-side and the french-door models. In the french- door style with two doors (often equally sized) that close to the middle and open outward in either direction, the top shelves are going to be harder for someone short, seated, or with limited range or motion to reach.

However, there are models available with either two separate bottom drawers or with a drawer within a drawer.

Often one of these drawers has the option of serving as a refrigerator compartment in addition to being set as a freezer. Set to the refrigerator mode, access would be available for people unable to reach higher shelves in the refrigerator.

Some cooktops have the controls on the surface along the front edge or in the lower corner of them. Induction cooktops have the touch controls along the front edge but on the surface of the cooktop.

Ranges (gas and electric) have their controls on the front facing out so they are easily accessible. As I mentioned in talking about contrast on page 100, some knobs are actually red.

Dishwashers are accessible to all — either the traditional model with the door opening down and the pull out baskets or the newer style with two drawers that open independently. They work well for someone in a wheelchair or seated.

As for appliances that need to be selected or installed with accessibility in mind, the oven when it is part of a range is fine. When the oven is mounted in the wall apart from the stove or range, it needs to be at a useable height.

Finding and selecting an oven with a side-opening door (hinged along the side rather than the bottom) provides more safety, convenience and accessibility than one that opens down. Just be aware of extra clearance that may be required for the door to open safely.

For double ovens, the top unit tends to be quite high for many people. Care should be taken to lower it and to make sure the controls and display are at eye-level or below.

Newer clothes dryers have the controls mounted on the front, but many older ones have them at the back.

Microwaves are often mounted in line with the cabinets over the range. They typically have a range hood/exhaust fan function built into them also. Because of where they are installed, they are difficult for many people to reach and use — especially reaching over a stove or cooktop that could be in use or seeing the controls well due the height of them.

People who are short, or those with range-of-motion or arm strength issues, face the additional challenge of removing hot food from the microwave and trying to set it down safely.

Some microwaves are installed with them directly resting on the countertop. While this brings them to a very useable and accessible level, countertop space is often forfeited.

Many homeowners and renters can replace appliances on their own or with the help of an installer from the store where the appliances are purchased.

Some professional assistance might be needed from a plumber, handyman, remodeler, or interior designer.

Wall Blocking

Wall blocking by itself — adding dimensional lumber (2" x 6", 2" x 8", 2" x 10", or 2" x 12") horizontally and flush between the vertical wall studs to provide material into which to anchor a future installation of grab bars or other devices — is not a universal design strategy.

However, it is an adaptable strategy that will facilitate the later installation of towel bars, grab bars, or other items that need to be anchored securely to the wall without being concerned about locating a stud or working with products that may not fit exactly where the studs are located. It also eliminates the need to rely on wall fasteners.

Using wider boards provides more flexibility in choosing an appropriate mounting height.

Using plywood sheathing (⅝" or ¾") across the studs will work, but it doesn't provide the thickness of 2" lumber (normally 1½" although labeled as 2" thick) and reduces the functional size of the room by its thickness since the drywall needs to go on top of it rather than applied directly to the wall studs as is the case with dimensional lumber blocking.

If you are doing your own remodeling, you can handle this. Otherwise, a handyman, carpenter, or remodeler can do this work.

Windows

Every home has windows, but there's a lot more to consider than just having them.

People generally select their home in part by the size and location of windows. They look for how well the windows add natural light to a space and how that varies throughout the day, the ability of the windows to provide ventilation and fresh air when they are opened, the view the windows offer from various rooms, how the windows might suggest furniture placement in a room (in a bedroom, family room, living room, dining room, or kitchen), and the way the size and shape of the windows fit into the exterior design.

Windows generally come with the home and are not specifically selected for how accessible they are or how easy they are to open. This often isn't discovered until after living in the home.

Some windows are not as accessible or easy to open as might have been thought once cabinetry or furniture is in front of them — partially blocking them or creating a barrier to reaching them.

Also, how far someone might need to reach, how much hand and arm strength they may need, or the range-of-motion required to push the window sash open or operate the crank are additional considerations that may not immediately come to mind.

Depending on what your local building codes require as a minimum height of a window from the floor, windows that provide easy viewing through them from a seated position are at a good height for everyone.

At such a height, anyone can access them as well for egress in an emergency and for emergency personnel to gain entry. This attribute of windows is often overlooked.

Thus, a relatively low window — in terms of distance of the sill from the floor — is a universal design feature because anyone can see through the glass and observe what is happening or enjoy the view.

The lower the windows are in relation to the floor, the easier they are going to be to open, but it's not just a matter of reaching the crank or the sash.

For safety, security, and comfort, the window needs to be latched securely.

For casement windows, the latch that secures the windows is usually located along the side of the window. Look for and select windows with the latch near the bottom or actually along the bottom rather than halfway up the side of the sash.

On single-hung and double-hung windows, the latching/locking mechanism is on top of the lower window sash or frame.

Sometimes security pins can be installed lower on the sash — in place of the lock at the top of the sash — by drilling through the sash and into the frame in one or more places to keep the window from opening or to keep it opened securely at a pre-determined amount.

Depending on the size of the windows, how high they are installed from the floor, how heavy they are, and how difficult they are to open and close, a short person, a child, someone in a wheelchair, someone with range-of-motion issues in their upper body, or someone without a lot of hand and arm strength may be unable to release or operate the windows.

Pay attention to the actual operation of opening the window once it is unlatched — the ease or difficulty in turning the crank to open a casement window or raising the lower sash of a single- or double-hung window.

Replacing windows is not a simple task, and professionals will need to be engaged to do this.

Adding impact resistance glass will be beneficial and universal also for safety and convenience — and peace of mind against possible intruders, mischief, vandalism, or wind storms.

Elevators

Elevators are in a class by themselves.

They aren't what we typically think of as a universal design feature, concept, or strategy, and they don't apply to ranch-style or single-level homes unless there is a basement.

Nevertheless, in multi-level homes they can be used by people that don't climb stairs well or by anyone else. In that sense, they are universal.

With two-story homes (or more), there may be a great opportunity for adaptable design by creating an elevator shaft for future use.

Maybe you already have a bedroom or hallway closet on each floor situated one on top of the other.

If not, look for the opportunity to design and create it.

It needs to be large enough for an elevator car so be sure to plan for this.

Then, whenever an elevator is desired, simply remove the ceiling of the first floor closet (which is the floor of the second floor closet) to create a cavity or shaft to house the elevator. Make sure that the landing and approach room is sufficient to operate the elevator.

The ceiling/floor that is being removed would be designed in such a way that it could be taken out for this purpose.

The closet doors can remain, but they should not interfere with getting on or off the elevator.

Even when it's not possible to align the two closets to create an elevator shaft, an elevator still might be a safety, comfort, convenient, and accessible design choice to include in a home for some people.

There also are elevators that can be installed outside the structure and attached and finished in such a way as to give the appearance that the home was designed and built with that feature included.

There are free-standing tubular elevators that can be used in spaces where a larger elevator wouldn't work or when a solution is desired without a lot of construction.

There are different primary energy sources available for elevators, but look for back-up batteries or how the unit can be powered by a back-up generator when there is a power outage.

Whatever solution you select in terms of an elevator, this is strictly a professional installation. A DME (durable medical equipment) supplier or consultant would be a good resource.

Chair Lifts

Like the elevator, having a chair lift applies to two-or-more-story homes or ones with a basement. There have to be stairs for this to work, and it's an alternative for moving people between floors.

Chair lifts themselves are not a universal design feature. Neither are platform lifts for people who need to be transported between levels (or even from the outside to the entrance of your home) while remaining in their wheelchairs.

Nevertheless, installing a chair lift may be desirable for someone who has moderate mobility, stamina, breathing, or balance issues.

The main consideration in putting in a chair lift — aside from the fact that there needs to be a stairway — is that someone can access the chair, sit in it as it climbs or descends stairs, and get off it safely because of range-of-motion issues (in their knees, hips, or ankles), stamina, balance, coordination, or cardio-vascular capacity.

The chair lift substitutes for the stairs or makes climbing them unnecessary while still being able to go up or down a floor.

An electric outlet located at the base of the stairs and the landing — even if not required by the building code — will mean that a chair lift could be installed at a future date if necessary or desired.

In the meantime, one can never have too many outlets. An outlet located here would facilitate plugging in decorative holiday lights and using the vacuum or other electrical appliances in this area of the home.

Just make sure that any type of remodeling that is done on or around the base of the stairs that sufficient floor space is maintained to accommodate the chair lift track. It rests on the floor and extends well past the base of the stairs.

If you are handy with home repairs, you could likely install this, but a professional can easily do it.

Back-Up Power

Aside from occasional power outages, storms can disrupt electricity for brief periods of time — from a few seconds to several hours or days.

While comfort, convenience, accessibility, and safety are important considerations during a power outage due to such items as alarm systems, lighting (interior and exterior), heating and air conditioning, computers, TVs, appliances, and refrigeration, some medically necessary equipment may depend on electricity as well.

While fuel oil, propane, or natural gas may power some items in the home such as hot water and heating, an electrical outage will shut off lights, TVs, computers, and refrigerators — at a minimum.

Back-up generators are quite useful and universal for supplying electrical power needs when the normal power service is interrupted — they just are not designed to take over the energy load of running your entire home because of the size of the generator that would be required and the amount of energy required to run it and keep it going.

Generators can power many essential and necessary systems, appliances, and items in your home — just not all of the energy needs in your home without a large, limitless, dependable power source.

Natural gas could be considered a large, limitless power source, but it can be quite expensive to run your entire house with it by powering your generator for several days.

If chair lifts, platform lifts, or elevators are present in your home — or you plan on installing them — they likely have back-up power designed into them. If not, the back-up generator would operate them.

Even a UPS (uninterruptible power supply) battery like you use for your computer can provide temporary backup for a few uses of a power bed or chair lift.

A back-up generator is something an electrician needs to install along with a remodeler or handyman so that it engages automatically when it is supposed to and powers those systems or devices that are important.

Installing the generator wrong could be an inefficient energy drain by running too many devices and very dangerous by backflowing power onto the electrical grid.

6

Universal Design On The Outside

Why Look At The Exterior?

In addition to all of the improvements, changes, modifications, strategies, and new installations you can make or have done on the inside of your home to create universal accessibility, safety, convenience, and comfort, there are many ways to improve the exterior of your home as well.

This applies whether you rent or own your home and whether it's a single family detached structure or a semi-attached/detached home such as a duplex, villa, or townhome.

Before you ever get inside your home or apartment, you need to have safe access and approach on the outside.

The principles of universal design and accessibility don't just magically begin once you or your visitors or guests open the front door and enter your living space.

They begin at the curb and continue along your entry sidewalks and driveway to the front door.

Here are a few ideas to get you started creating an accessible and safe living environment from the outside-in.

Zero-Step/Barrier-Free Entrances

In some parts of the country, building codes may not allow a true zero-step entrance into your home that is at grade level.

However, there may other ways to accomplish this through a gentle sloping or ramping that bridges the few inches that the threshold needs to be above grade for flooding concerns or other issues.

Whatever the local building codes require or allow in terms of making a zero-step threshold or entry — or prohibiting it — must be followed.

The concept of a zero-step or barrier free entry is to allow anyone easy, unrestricted access to your home, whether it's you, other household members, your guests or your visitors (invited or not) — from young to old and walking unaided, using a walker or wheelchair, being pushed in a baby carriage or stroller, using a wheeled toy, or just having a range-of-motion issue that makes stepping up and down difficult.

Nevertheless, everyone will need to step on or over the wooden or metal threshold against which the entry door closes, but the concept of barrier free is to reduce and eliminate other steps and barriers along the entry walk — from the driveway or street to the entrance of your home.

In some cases, an attractive, well-constructed, and well-landscaped ramp may be used as universal access to your home — or in addition to steps or another type of approach that might be present.

Such ramps provide an alternative entry without necessarily calling attention to its presence and may be used whether they are required for accessibility or not.

Lighting

Beginning on page 38, I discuss photo cells, timers, and motion sensors.

These all work outside as well as indoors provided they can withstand the elements or are used in a relatively dry or covered area (such as on a porch or covered entry, or under the eaves or overhang).

Another type of lighting that can be used outdoors is a solar powered one.

It can be a yard or house light that stays on all night or one that just comes on when it detects motion – depending on what type of light is selected and what the objective is.

The principal advantage to this type of light is that it can be located anywhere on the property because it does not need to be wired into or plugged into electricity.

It draws its energy from batteries that are recharged by the sun.

Of course, the solar collector that recharges the batteries needs to be in a place where it can receive sunlight.

Locate it away from tree branches or other objects that might block the sunlight from reaching the solar collector.

Entry Shelves/Tables/Furniture

A universal design strategy that definitely appeals to all ages and abilities and addresses safety, comfort, convenience, and accessibility issues is an outdoor entry shelf or piece of furniture such as a table.

This is installed or placed next to the entrance (the latch side or door handle side of the front door — unless you use the side door or back door as much or more than the front door and it can apply to these doors also).

The shelf, table, stand, or other piece of furniture should be somewhat lower in height than the door handle so as not to interfere with its function and safe operation.

You can use most any dimension that you like, but it should be large enough and deep enough to be functional without be so big that it is obtrusive or a barrier to entering safely.

Depending on its size and shape, it might provide storage space inside or underneath it or allow for a small sculpture or plant on top.

It can be wood or metal and can be painted, stained, or decorated as you like to be compatible with the general design, theme, and colors of your home or entry porch.

It's quite common to get out of the car and walk up to the front door with your hands full of various things.

This may not be an all-the-time occurrence, but often you might be carrying the mail, an umbrella, a jacket that you aren't wearing, groceries, packages, shopping bags, books, tools, dry cleaning, a briefcase, purse, toddlers, a cup of coffee or a soft drink, fast food (that you are still eating or in the bag to eat once inside), or a cell phone.

Maybe you are trying to assist someone else to get into your home or show attention to a pet that greets you.

Then, with your hands full of what you are carrying or attending to, you need to look for your keys, make or take a phone call, keep from dropping something you have been carrying that is beginning to slip, or have a hand free to open the door.

Having a shelf or object (such as a table or stand) to set things on makes perfect sense rather than juggling them, trying to balance them, or setting them on the ground.

Just make sure that whatever you decide to use — a shelf, cabinet, stand, table, or other object or piece of furniture —that it is painted or otherwise treated to withstand precipitation if it is in an area that might get wet (directly or from windblown rain or snow).

Covered Entry/Guttering

When you arrive at your front door — or you have guests or visitors that come to your front door — it should be dry even if it is snowing or raining right up until you or your guests arrive at the door.

This is a safety, comfort, and convenience solution that definitely appeals to all ages and abilities.

You and your guests or visitors need to be sheltered from rain or snow when it is present so you can pause in a dry area immediately before entering your home without being subjected to the precipitation.

This gives you and your visitors time to compose yourself as you shake off the rain or snow, take off your raincoat, clean off your boots or shoes, or shake off and fold up your umbrella – whether you first have to unlock the door or just open it and enter.

Most entrances have an overhang of sorts, but at a minimum guttering should be installed to keep the precipitation from running off the roof and onto you or your guests – generally at a fairly heavy flow – when you or they approach the door.

It also – if it is installed correctly – will collect and drain the water away from the sidewalk or driveway that you and your guests will use to approach the front door – keeping everyone's feet dryer and providing safer, surer footing on the walkway and more accessibility without having to navigate around puddles or slippery spots on the walkway.

A covered entry or porch (that also has guttering along the edge of it for the reasons just mentioned) provides even more protection and shelter.

Then with the entry shelf, stand, table, or other piece of furniture I mentioned, you can set down anything you are holding while you open the door.

You might be able to install the guttering that you get from the home center store.

However, a covered entry is likely a job for a handyman, carpenter, or remodeler — possibly an architect or roofer if it is particularly large or will be tied into the existing roofline.

Radiant Heating

In areas where temperatures are cold enough for ice and snow to be present, a universal design feature and treatment that provides safety, comfort, convenience, and accessibility is radiant heating in the concrete sidewalks (front, back, and side), driveways, and patios around the home so that the ice and snow are melted and the possibility of slipping or having unsure footing is greatly reduced or eliminated.

This also will keep wet patches of melted snow or ice or other precipitation (rain or sleet) from freezing when the temperature drops low enough.

This obviously is a major renovation project and will require the services of people such as a remodeler, flatwork contractor, HVAC contractor, cement mason, architect, and landscape architect to produce an attractive, effective result.

Unloading/Landing Area

Where two-car driveways are wide enough to accommodate people unloading from a vehicle without stepping in the grass, dirt, or planting area along the sides of the driveway, no other work may be desired.

Generally, this would only be true if the vehicle was parked to the left side of the driveway with the right side being used for the loading area.

For single-car driveways, this universal design solution should be implemented.

For increased safety, convenience, comfort and accessibility, the driveway — regardless of its current width (but definitely for single-car driveways) — should be enlarged along the right side of the driveway (facing it from the street) with a hard, all-weather surface of concrete or pavers to allow plenty of firm footing for all passengers to disembark from their vehicle (wherever it is parked on the driveway) and to allow plenty of space for a walker or wheelchair to be unloaded, set up, and used.

This extra loading and unloading space is beneficial for everyone — especially on inclement days or when the vehicle needs to be loaded with luggage, supplies, schoolwork, pets, or other objects in addition to the occupants of the vehicle.

For vans with ramps that extend from the vehicle (to allow people in wheelchairs or those with other mobility issues to safely enter and exit the vehicle), there needs to be space for the ramp to deploy and for people to still be on a hard surface while entering or after leaving the van.

Everything that holds true for your household members would also apply to visitors and guests.

When not needed for passenger unloading or loading, the extra driveway space can be used for parking (cars, motorcycles, golf carts, or bicycles), as a seating area with lawn chairs, or as a play area.

The extra width can be just as practical when not needed for getting in and out of the vehicles which is why this is a universal design and visitable strategy.

Sidewalks

Many homes are built without much attention to the sidewalks leading from the street to the front door or from the driveway to the front door.

Sometimes a basic walkway is formed and poured — or one is created with brick pavers — without much attention to function.

Some homes don't even have a formal sidewalk — they just have a path, with or without stepping stones. The dirt path can become muddy, and those with stepping stones can become overgrown with grass and difficult to use because of the spacing between them or the fact that they are broken or pitched in various directions.

Many dirt paths and hard surface sidewalks retain water during a rain or lawn sprinkling.

Some walkways have intermediate steps and may or may not have railings for assistance.

A much more strategic — and visible — approach to the sidewalk is to make it wide enough for easy use by children playing, for people using a walker or wheelchair, for moving furniture or equipment in and out of the home, or for two or more people to walk side-by-side (together or coming and going) on the walkway.

Also take into account creating a non-slip surface (under most conditions), the rise and slope of the walkway (eliminating steps whenever possible), installing it slightly above grade for better drainage (if the building code allows it), and making it easy to use in terms of twists and turns. There might even need to be one or more flat intermediate landings.

Also, the landscaping and other obstacles along the walkway is an important safety consideration to keep in mind with the possibility of someone veering from the hard surface.

Designing, forming, pouring, and finishing your walkway is something for the professionals to do — landscape architect, flatwork contractor, cement finisher, remodeler, occupational therapist, architect, or handyman.

Remember to include your radiant heating in your sidewalk remodeling plans unless you are in a warm climate.

7

Summary Of Universal Design Treatments

Universal Design Makes A Positive Difference

I've been showing you various options, ideas, and solutions that are available to you to improve your home and add to the overall lifestyle and enjoyment of everyone who lives in your home.

This is the concept of universal design — making your living space (inside and out) as comfortable, convenient, safe, accessible, and enjoyable as possible for everyone living in your home as well as people who are just visiting.

Those visits could be just an hour or two for someone just dropping by or attending a function you are hosting, or they could be for a few days for overnight guests. In the case of visiting family, those stays could be longer than a week.

In addition to quality improvements that you get to see and experience in your home, universal design changes and treatments also add value to your home that you will realize when you go to sell it in the future.

Without an appraisal, there is no way to put a specific dollar amount on how much the value of your home will be improved with your universal design changes, but the fact that it literally will appeal to the broadest of audiences makes it generally desirable and worth more. It likely will sell quicker as a result.

An additional objective in universal design is to make the changes and treatments as invisible as possible so that they don't stand out or call attention to themselves except as something high tech, modern, or interesting to use.

People shouldn't notice that anything special has been done to accommodate or adapt your home for special needs unless that was your intent.

As far as making your home more livable, safe, and enjoyable, the design features that I have been suggesting to you will accomplish those objectives and fit right in as good design elements.

Universal Design Helps With Special Needs

There are plenty of special needs modifications that can be made to serve and address specific situations.

However, this text has focused on those design changes, improvements, solutions, and treatments that can impact and accommodate everyone in your home regardless of their age, physical size, strength, or abilities.

If you have special needs in your home that you specifically need to accommodate — or you might in the near future — you should find the universal design suggestions that I have presented in this book as quite helpful and a great place to start.

Universal design features — if they truly are designed for all ages and abilities — will let people with certain mobility, sensory, or cognitive issues function quite well in their surroundings the same as people without those concerns.

That's why these features are called universal design, and that's the big benefit of using them. They let essentially everyone live better in their homes.

They allow you to appeal to basically everyone who lives in your home or visits you with good, comfortable, safe, accessible, intuitive, easy-to-use design choices in such areas of your home as lighting, controls, doors, cabinets, mirrors, faucets, shelving, appliances, entrances, walkways, passageways, flooring, and bathroom fixtures.

However, if you need to install or design a solution beyond what I have presented here, an occupational therapist, physical therapist, DME (durable medical equipment) consultant, or other health care professional (HCP) should be consulted to create a specific functional design.

Even with that, universal design treatments will still serve them well in the other areas of your home.

Universal Design Adds Value And Enjoyment

Whether the universal design changes in and around your home are made by you as the homeowner or tenant, or you call in or consult professionals to manage or accomplish the work, those strategies and solutions will make your life easier and more enjoyable.

Your home and living space will be safer to use.

The items that have been addressed and presented in this text will enable you and those who live with you or visit you to use your living space more effectively and comfortably as well.

You will be increasing the level of comfort, convenience, and accessibility while reducing the potential for injury, frustration, or unnecessary effort.

You, and the others in your home, will have an easier time of seeing, reaching, and using various controls, fixtures, and appliances.

When the changes, solutions, strategies, and methods that have been presented in this text are employed, the immediate result will be the increased enjoyment of your home.

The longer term benefit will be the added value in terms of desirability for future owners.

Resale value should be enhanced because the changes will increase the appeal and broaden the potential purchaser base to a much larger audience.

As much as you look forward to making some, most, or all of the changes to your home that have been presented here, just think of how much someone else might like to find a home that already has made these changes for them.

Now, It's Up To You

The universal design concepts, treatments, solutions, tips, recommendations, and strategies that I have presented in this book for you are intended to be used by you to impact and increase the accessibility, safety, comfort, convenience, value (marketability), and visitability of your living space.

Perhaps you can tackle many of these projects yourself. If not, you now know what can be done and how to talk with professionals who can help you achieve the results that you seek.

Now, it's up to you to determine where you want to begin as you start incorporating these features into your home, apartment, or design projects.

You may already have some of these completed. That's a great start, and now you can add to what's already been done.

Begin to prioritize what you want to do, determine which (if any) of the projects you want to do yourself, and then reach out to professionals who can help you with the rest.

I'm available as a resource for you also.

Steve Hoffacker

Steve Hoffacker, AICP, CAASH, CAPS, CGA, CGP, CMP, CSP, MCSP, MIRM, is principal of Hoffacker Associates LLC, a new home sales training and real estate coaching company based in West Palm Beach, Florida.

Steve is an award-winning new home sales trainer and coach, commercial real estate broker, marketing consultant, award-winning photographer, best-selling author, blogger, teacher, and salesman.

For more than 30 years, he has helped homebuilders, new home salespeople, Realtors®, small business owners, and other professional salespeople to be more visible, competitive, profitable, and effective — and to really enjoy themselves as they pursue their business.

He has embraced the concept of universal design and has given you many examples of how to incorporate them into your existing home — as part of normal maintenance and updating or through a larger scale remodeling project.

He interacts with providers from around North America in his classes and has incorporated many of these treatments into his own home so he speaks from practical experience.

Many of the suggestions Steve provides in this book are printed here for the first time. You won't find them anywhere else as of this printing.

www.ingramcontent.com/pod-product-compliance
Lightning Source LLC
Chambersburg PA
CBHW071609170426
43196CB00034B/2251